S·E·R·V·E·S
12
UNLESS ROY'S INVITED
SOUTHERN RECIPES AT THEIR BEST

Lynda Harrill

A PERIGEE BOOK

Perigee Books
are published by
The Putnam Publishing Group
200 Madison Avenue
New York, NY 10016

Designed by Rhea Braunstein

Library of Congress Cataloging-in-Publication Data
Harrill, Lynda, date.
Serves 12 unless Roy's invited / Lynda Harrill.
p. cm.
ISBN 0-399-51617-4
1. Cookery, American—Southern style. I. Title. II. Title:
Serves twelve unless Roy's invited.
Includes index.
TX715.2.S68H37 1990
641.5975—dc20   89-48847
CIP

Printed in the United States of America
1 2 3 4 5 6 7 8 9 10

Contents

Acknowledgments   5

Introduction   7

Cooking Essentials   11

Roy's Favorites   16

Pork   17

Poultry   31

Seafood   47

Beef and Veal   63

Rice and Grits   75

Vegetables   87

Appetizers   103

Salads   113

Soups and Stews   123

Breads   133

Desserts   141

Index   153

Acknowledgments

When I bailed out of the corporate world to pursue entrepreneurial interests, I intended to start a consulting business specializing in strategic planning and marketing. (I may get there yet!) I decided to take some time off first to relax, have some fun and get a few projects done around the house. My husband, Roy, suggested I use some of this down time to organize my recipes. He had just bought a new personal computer and wanted me to try out the new software. I would need word processing and desktop publishing skills in my consulting business, so I decided to practice on my recipes. Next thing I knew, I was in the middle of a full-scale cookbook project.

My family and friends were very supportive. Momma and Aunt Mamie provided invaluable technical assistance and many wonderful recipes. My neighbors, Brenda, Barb and Connie, were willing tasters and testers. Roy's kids, Dawn, Wendy and Jon, offered moral support from the East Coast and volunteered for tasting duties—just send them a plane ticket and they'd eat our food—for free!

My dear friend Mary inspired the cookbook's title. One day I prepared two batches of Mary's Special Chicken for a dinner party with 16 guests. One batch normally serves 12, so I figured I was safe in doubling it. I planned to freeze the leftovers, but I had only about two bites left. Roy was the guest of honor.

My penultimate thank you goes to Roy—barbeque aficionado, fried chicken fanatic, shrimp devotee and my biggest fan. He's a tireless taster and constructive critic. He's a wonderful husband and pretty good at editing cookbooks.

Finally, I thank God that I was born and raised in Charleston, South Carolina, and that I was able to publish Roy's favorite recipes for others to enjoy.

Introduction

When it comes to eating, my husband, Roy, makes Tommy Lasorda look like a rookie. He'd even give Willard Scott a good run for his money. He's a Southern food fanatic for sure, although his looks don't show it. The man just loves to eat and I just love to cook, so we're a match made in Heaven . . . Hog Heaven!

Keeping a Southern food fanatic satisfied is a full-time job yet a very rewarding experience. Whoever said the way to a man's heart is through his stomach really understood male anatomy, especially Roy's.

The Early Years

It all started when I left Charleston, South Carolina, for a semester in my junior year of college, as a History exchange student in England. The food (if you can call it that) was just short of dreadful. I lost ten pounds in two weeks and figured I had to do something before Momma had to fly over to claim the body. Luckily, my dormitory had a fully equipped kitchen, so I began to experiment. It's always struck me as ironic that I learned how to cook out of self-defense.

After college, I started to spread my culinary wings. I became an expert in green beans with Durkee fried onions, ground beef in golden mushroom soup, beef Stroganoff and chicken divan. Seems every dish had some sort of sauce. After a while, they all tasted like "cream of something" soup to me. It wasn't until Momma gave me my first copy of *Charleston Receipts* that I really fell in love with cooking. I started collecting cookbooks. I wanted to appreciate a variety of cuisines. My kitchen became my laboratory. My friends became willing guinea pigs. Cooking became my passion when I met Roy.

Enter a Southern Food Fanatic

I met Roy eleven years ago. It was love at first sight—even before he knew I could cook and I knew he could eat, and I do mean eat. Then it was love at first bite. A little Red Rice, Meeting Street Crab, Shrimp and Grits, Barbeque and Chicken went a long way toward building our relationship. Then when he discovered Bessinger's Barbeque on his first visit to Charleston, I knew he was mine.

I can't accept responsibility for making Roy a Southern food fanatic, but I've certainly helped maintain a condition he developed in early childhood. Roy's love of good food is truly amazing. He's a culinary legend among our family and friends. He's even replaced Charlie Johnson, my grandmother's old gardener, as the all-time eating champion in the largest-single-serving and multiple-servings competition. Seems like no matter how much I cook, he always has room for more.

Let Your Stomach Plan Your Vacation

Every summer for the past ten years, Roy and I have driven from Chicago to the Washington, D.C., area and then on to Charleston to visit our families. We navigate based on barbeque establishments and other restaurants known for their fried chicken. Roy takes this all very seriously. He has only two weeks each year to fill up on those things that make a fanatic think he's died and gone straight to Heaven. We have many tough decisions to make—should we go to Parker's in Wilson or Wilber's in Goldsboro for barbeque? Since we usually can't do both, we've had some great debates. While we fill ourselves, we also fill the trunk of the car with cherished Southern provisions—bottles and bottles of our favorite regional barbeque sauces, Mrs. Sassard's relishes and pickles, benne seed cookies, dried cow peas, golden grits, etc.—to tide us over during those cold Midwest winters. For two weeks each year, Roy experiences true culinary ecstasy, then he diets for the next six weeks.

Satisfying a Southern Food Fanatic

This book will help you gain control of a Southern food fanatic's appetite. I've written down less 'en a cuppa hunnert (that's Charleston Geechee talk for approximately 140) of Roy's favorite recipes. They are guaranteed to satisfy anyone who enjoys traditional Southern cooking with a gourmet touch. Even if you don't have a fanatic in the family (yet), you'll find some good, healthful eating described in the following pages. Some recipes are quick and easy, ones I usually prepare during the week on "school nights." Others require a little more time, and are best saved to prepare on those rainy weekend afternoons or Saturday mornings before the rest of the household stirs. You can make multiple batches and load up your freezer. Remember, living with a Southern food fanatic requires some advance preparation.

Next Steps

Before you jump ahead to the recipes, I'd suggest you browse through "Cooking Essentials." It contains a list of things you should accumulate so you can fully enjoy the recipes. You may need to add a few of these items to your Christmas list this year.

Now It's Your Turn

I hope you'll enjoy preparing Roy's favorites and eating them as much as Roy and I have. Who knows, you may get to create a Southern food fanatic. Good cookin' and good luck!

LYNDA HARRILL

May 1990

COOKING ESSENTIALS

Southern cooking, Charleston cooking in particular, requires a few special items. You may already own some of them. Many are available just about anywhere. Some require a little imagination and improvisation or a few phone calls to South Carolina. I'll provide details later.

Rice Steamers

You can never have too many rice steamers. I have five! They ensure perfectly steamed rice every time and they're great for steaming vegetables too. Wear-Ever makes my favorite steamer. The Foley Company also makes a nice steamer. Steamers are usually available in kitchen specialty shops and hardware stores.

Moha Mandolin

This is an indispensable instrument. Julienned vegetables and paper-thin slices of vegetables and fruits are prepared with little effort. Just watch out for your fingers. The blade is very sharp. You should be able to find this universal grater in kitchen specialty shops.

Cast Iron Skillet

You'll need one of these to prepare "blackened" foods. A traditional round skillet holds four servings, so I'd also recommend buying a large rectangular cast iron griddle for larger crowds.

Blender

Generally, I don't believe in "powered assistance" (you'll see no call for microwaves or food processors in this book). I do, however, make a few exceptions. A good blender is one of them.

Hand Mixer

All right, I finally broke down and bought one. It was whipping cream by hand that finally did me in. While I prefer a wire whisk, it's just not enough for some recipes.

Dried Spices

You should make sure you have these spices on hand before you begin cooking. There's nothing more frustrating than reaching for a particular spice while you're in the middle of preparation, only to find you don't have any. A few frantic trips to the grocery cured me of this kind of forgetfulness.

Allspice	Chili powder
Basil	Chinese red peppers
Bay leaves	Cinnamon
Benne seeds (sesame)	Cloves
Black peppercorns	Cumin
Cayenne	Curry powder
Celery seed	Dill weed

Fennel	Oregano
Filé	Paprika
Garlic powder	Parsley
Ginger	Red pepper flakes
Green peppercorns	Rosemary
Lavender	Sage
Mace	Tarragon
Marjoram	Thyme
Nutmeg	Turmeric
Onion powder	White peppercorns

Ready-Made Products

Be sure to have this next list of products in your pantry. Some of these could never be duplicated. How would you like to try to make your own Worcestershire sauce from scratch? All are a must for your kitchen!

Hellmann's mayonnaise
Durkee Famous Sauce
Colman's dry mustard
Lea & Perrins Worcestershire sauce
Tabasco sauce
Puritan oil
Kitchen Bouquet

Wyler's instant bouillon, chicken and beef flavors
Progresso tomato paste
Progresso bread crumbs—Italian style
Quaker Oats Quick Golden Grits
Liquid Smoke
Karo syrup (dark and light)
Mrs. Sassard's artichoke and sweet onion relishes, iced tomato pickles and pickled artichokes.*
Old El Paso Taco Sauce (hot)

When You're in a Hurry

I also keep the following on hand for those times when I don't have the time to cook certain items from scratch. They are dependable brand-name products and come very close to "homemade" when added to certain recipes.

Pepperidge Farm Herb Seasoned Stuffing
Boucanier Barbecue sauce*
K.C. Masterpiece Barbecue Sauce
Maurice's Gourmet Barbeque Sauces*
Melvin's Southern Barbecue sauce*

*These items can be ordered by mail. See "Charleston Favorites" and "Other Favorites" for addresses.

Wisconsin Wilderness Barbecue sauces*
Betty Crocker walnut brownie mix

Charleston Favorites

Charleston favorites are available as follows:

Mrs. Sassard's relishes, etc.—call (803) 884-4574 or write: 443 Church Street, Mt. Pleasant, SC 29464

Melvin's Southern Barbecue sauce—call (803) 556-1354 or write: 1602 Savannah Highway, Charleston, SC 29407

Other Favorites

Boucanier Barbecue sauce—call (800) 253-3663 or write: A Southern Season, Eastgate, Chapel Hill, NC 27514

Maurice's Gourmet Barbeque Sauces—call (800) MAURICE or write: P. O. Box 6847, West Columbia, SC 29171

Wisconsin Wilderness Barbecue sauces—call (414) 355-0001 or write: 7841 N. 47th Street, Milwaukee, WI 53223

Other Provisions

I don't prefer any particular brand, but you'll need to keep these things on hand too. Some are available in low-calorie versions.

Bacon	Olive oil
Brown rice	Red wine
Brown sugar	Red wine vinegar
Butter	Sherry
Cornstarch	Soy sauce
Cow peas (dried field peas)	Sweet and sour sauce
Hoisin sauce	Teriyaki sauce
Italian dressing	White rice
Margarine	White wine
Marsala wine	

Outside Necessities

Covered Grill

You'll need a covered grill—either charcoal or gas. Actually you'd be better off with both if you can manage it. I sometimes use a charcoal grill to smoke meat and then finish the cooking over low heat on my gas grill. I highly recommend a Weber grill. I'm on my second Weber kettle since 1974. Then I discovered gas grills. I am starting on my fifth season with my Weber Genesis II. I cook everything I possibly can on the grill. All kinds of meat and vegetables. And even though we have very harsh winters (nothing like a 75-degrees-below-zero wind chill to discourage outdoor cooking), I cook outside all year round. When it snows, the grill is the first thing we dig out. We have our priorities!

Hickory Chips

If you like smoky flavors, hickory chips are a must. These can be bought in most supermarkets, butcher shops and where grills are sold. Soak chips in water for 20 to 30 minutes, drain well and place directly on hot coals. When chips start smoking, it's time to cook.

If you use a gas grill, you can put the chips on the hot lava rocks. If you own a Weber Genesis, buy a Steam-N-Chips Smoker™ attachment or place the chips into a small disposable aluminum pan and put the pan in far left corner of the preheated grill.

Charcoal Rails

You'll need to invest in some charcoal rails to make indirect cooking easier. They keep the briquets to the sides when you want to cook not char the meat.

Other Cookbooks

As much as I hate to promote the competition, there are a few cookbooks you may want to add to your collection.

Huguenin, M.V., and Stoney, A.M., eds. *Charleston Receipts*. Charleston, SC: Junior League of Charleston, SC, 1950.

Logan, Eunice S., and Speights, Elizabeth L. *Charleston Receipts Repeats*. Charleston, SC: Junior League of Charleston, SC, 1986.

McCoin, Choice, ed. *300 Years of Carolina Cooking*. Greenville, SC: Junior League of Greenville, SC, 1970.

Wilson, Justin. *The Justin Wilson Gourmet and Gourmand Cookbook*. Gretna, LA: Pelican, 1984.

Wilson, Justin. *Justin Wilson's Outdoor Cooking with Inside Help*. Gretna, LA: Pelican, 1986.

Junior League of Baton Rouge, Inc., Staff, eds. *River Road Recipes*. Baton Rouge, LA: Junior League of Baton Rouge, LA, 1985.

McKee, Gwen. *Little Gumbo Book: Twenty-Seven Carefully Created Recipes That Will Enable Everyone to Enjoy the Special Experience of Gumbo*. Brandon, MS: Quail Ridge Press, 1986.

Davis, Rick, and Stein, Shifra. *The All-American Barbecue Book*. New York: Random House, 1988.

Johnson, Greg. *Real Barbecue*. New York: Harper & Row, 1988.

Roy's Favorites

Roy says **all** the recipes in this book are wonderful; however, there are some small differences. He realizes you may not be able to try every recipe, so after much deliberation he's devised a rating system to identify what he calls "the best of the best."

Look for one little "pig" after a recipe. This signifies "the best of the best," meaning you can't die and go to Heaven till you've tasted it.

PORK

Many Southerners will say pork is the meat of choice in the South, although fried chicken fans might argue the point. Chicken *is* good, but pork is very special and its preparation reflects quite a bit of Southern tradition and family pride. Pork chops, roasts, tenderloin and ribs are popular, but nothing can compete with a Southerner's love of "barbeque."

"Southern barbeque," as this style of pork is called, is a true labor of love. Pork shoulders or whole hogs are cooked ever so slowly, 10 to 14 hours over very low heat, in open pits. Fires are built of wood—usually hickory or oak. Some pits have been modernized to use natural gas. There are even a few electric pits. There's always a great debate about the best cooking method. Barbeque purists shudder at the mere thought of using anything but wood. The pits and meat require constant attention to ensure the barbeque will be consistently moist and flavorful. The cooked meat is either shredded or chopped, then mixed with barbeque sauce. Sauce recipes are closely guarded family secrets.

Barbeque is a true Southern delight and has become a Southern art form.

Roy would do anything for some good ole Southern barbeque. When his daughter Wendy moved to North Carolina he was delighted with the prospect of receiving regular shipments of his beloved smoky shredded pork via Federal Express. She lived in Greensboro and then Raleigh, so Roy had several different tastes of regional North Carolina barbeque. When Wendy moved, Roy was distraught that his North Carolina barbeque connection was gone. But

Momma still flies up from Charleston on occasion with a little South Carolina barbeque—usually Melvin's—tucked under her arm. It's always carried on the plane, never checked. O'Hare couldn't handle the ensuing riot if Roy's Southern barbeque were to go astray in lost luggage.

Barbeque Syntax

It's a verb . . . it's a noun . . . it's an adjective . . . it's barbeque!

Barbeque is one of those words that can cause great confusion. If I could speak to you personally, you'd probably understand the differences in meaning rather quickly. If I let you taste some barbeque, you'd understand instantly. But, I've got to write this down, so it'll take a little longer.

Barbeque, the verb—to prepare food on an outdoor grill. (Not just pork, but also chicken, fish, shellfish, beef, lamb, vegetables, even pizza.)
Barbeque, the noun—pork roasts cooked very slowly usually over hickory wood or chips, chopped, shredded or sliced and covered with your barbeque sauce of choice.
Barbeque, the other noun—one or more hungry Southerners gathered for the express purpose of eating barbeque.
Barbeque, the other, other noun—the cooking apparatus used to prepare barbeque.
Barbeque, the adjective—possessing the quality of having been cooked on the grill and/or having been coated with barbeque sauce near the end of cooking. Technically it should be "barbequed," but we seldom write or pronounce the "d."

One more item of syntax requires some clarification. You'll see *barbeque* spelled many different ways—barbeque, barbecue, Bar-B-Cue, Bar-B-Que, Bar-B-Q, B-B-Q, BBQ—depending on factors such as the region of the South you're from, personal preference or your spelling ability. Don't let the spelling differences bother you; they all mean great eating.

Southern Barbeque—Where to Find It

The ultimate way to enjoy pork barbeque is to head South; but since that may not always be possible, you'll need to know how to make a little barbeque to tide you over until you can get your Southern trip organized. You'll be a backyard Southern barbeque expert in no time with my recipe for Do-It-Yourself Southern Barbeque.

If you can manage a trip, you'll need to know a few things to get you started. First, the variation in the regional barbeques is truly amazing. No matter where you start, you can't go wrong. They're all wonderful, they're all different. Eating real Southern barbeque is a heavenly delight. It's totally impossible to choose an absolute Number 1 favorite. At least that's what Roy says. So each year we go in search of the elusive best barbeque. We drive from Chicago to Charleston on quiet Southern backroads visiting friends and looking for barbeque places we haven't yet tried. In two weeks, Roy usually manages to eat barbeque at least fourteen times (sometimes including breakfast), so we get a chance to sample a wide variety.

Another thing to keep in mind is that Southern barbeque is traditionally served with other Southern specialties. Most restaurants serve family-style (all-you-can-eat, served at the table) dinners that include Southern Fried Chicken (p. 42), Brunswick Stew (p. 129), Corn Bread (p. 137), Hush Puppies (p. 139), cole slaw, boiled new potatoes, black-eyed peas, corn on the cob, and green beans with their barbeque. Maurice's Piggie Park serves a delicious pork hash over rice. His brother Melvin makes wonderful gigantic onion rings (you can eat 'em or use 'em as spare tires). Parker's cornbread sticks are outstanding as is their cole slaw. The Rib Cage's version of Banana Pudding (p. 150) provides the perfect ending to an all-you-can-eat, eat-till-you-drop Southern barbeque pigout. They serve great barbeque ribs too! So don't eat anything for at least two weeks before you head South.

If you're really interested in the lore of barbeque, two books devoted to barbeque cover good barbeque eating all over the United States: *Real Barbecue* (Harper & Row) and *The All-American Barbecue Book* (Vintage Press) provide insight into the barbeque mystique—preparation, accompaniments and secret sauces. They also provide names, complete addresses and directions to several hundred wonderful barbeque establishments. These books are invaluable reference sources.

Roy says the best way to find good barbeque is to ask, and experience shows this to be very true. We ask people such as local residents in the Barbeque Belt, fellow travelers at motels and rest stops along the highways, other diners in restaurants and Southern business associates. I even learned about a new barbeque spot when I called North Carolina to order furniture. We've found some of the most delicious barbeque by asking total strangers for their recommendations. It's a natural topic of conversation in the South, so don't be shy.

Finally, be sure your travels include a stop at as many of the barbeque haunts listed here as you can. These are our favorites. Eat all the barbeque and fixings your stomach allows and buy some of the sauce to take home to your "barbeque sauce cellar." Back at home you can concentrate on cooking the pork just right and use some of the delicious ready-made sauces. If you can't stop in, most places will ship you sauce. Some will even ship you the barbeque too! You can call 1-800-MAURICE for his "Flying Pig Service."

SOUTH CAROLINA

Charleston	Melvin's/Bessinger's
	The Rib Cage
Summerville	Droze's
Beaufort	Duke's
Holly Hill	Sweatman's
Orangeburg	Duke's
Columbia	Maurice's Piggie Park
	Millender's
Leesville	Shealy's
Elgin	Hammy's

NORTH CAROLINA

Goldsboro	Wilber's
	Scott's
Wilson	Parker's
	Bill's
Greensboro	Stamey's
Lexington	Lexington #1
Raleigh	Barbecue Lodge

VIRGINIA

Newport News	Rocky Mount Bar-B-Q
Williamsburg	Pierce's

TENNESSEE

Newport	'Shiners

KENTUCKY

Owensboro	Moonlight Bar-B-Q Inn

INDIANA

Schererville	Hickory Smokehouse

Do-It-Yourself Southern Barbeque

Get ready for one of the most rewarding experiences of your life. Yes, you're gonna invest a little time in this process, but wait till you see the faces of your family and friends when they bite into this treat. Allow at least 2 pounds per person when buying pork roasts. They'll make pigs of themselves! This freezes extremely well, so as long as you're going to all the trouble, make a huge batch. Serve with Red Rice (p. 79), Charleston Squash Pie (p. 91), cole slaw and a little of Mrs. Sassard's artichoke relish. You'll be addicted for sure! Barbeque makes great sandwiches too!

SERVES 8 TO 10.

15 lbs. boneless pork roasts (3 lbs. each)
2 cups hickory chips
3 cups Carolina Gold (p. 22)

Start an indirect charcoal fire in your Weber kettle. (Use charcoal rails or put a rectangular pan under the center of the grill on the coal rack and put the charcoal along the outside.) Soak hickory chips in water for 30 minutes then drain well. When the coals are ashen gray, cover them with one half the hickory chips and put pork roasts on middle of the grill. Cook for 30 minutes, add remaining hickory chips and cook another 15 minutes.

Preheat gas grill or oven to 250 degrees. Cook roasts until meat thermometer registers 165 degrees, about 30 to 45 minutes.

Slice roasts into 2-inch chunks. Shred meat with two large meat forks into large bite-size pieces. (You'll build up your forearms doing this.) Place shredded pork into large pot and mix with 2 cups Carolina Gold. Heat through, adding more sauce as it is absorbed. Serve with extra sauce.

TIP The secret to moist pork is slow cooking, so don't make your kettle fire too hot. Use only 8 or 10 briquets on each side. If the fire looks too hot, remove the roasts and spritz the coals till they calm down, then resume cooking.

Carolina Gold

If you like to make your own barbeque sauces, you'll enjoy adding this one to your repertoire. It's mustard-based, not the standard tomato-based sauce that dominates barbeque saucedom. In South Carolina, from Charleston to Columbia, mustard-based sauces are the norm. Even Roy was skeptical at first. But after just one taste, he knew he had found "barbeque sauce heaven." If you don't have time to prepare your own, Melvin's or Maurice's mustard-based sauces will do just fine.

MAKES ABOUT 2 CUPS.

> 1½ cups French's prepared mustard
> 5 tbsp. brown sugar
> 4 tbsp. tomato paste
> 3 tbsp. apple cider vinegar
> 1 tbsp. Worcestershire sauce
> ½ tsp. cayenne
> ½ tsp. black pepper
> ½ tsp. garlic powder

Combine all ingredients in a saucepan and simmer for about 5 minutes to dissolve sugar. Remove from heat and let cool before using.

Refrigerate leftover sauce in an airtight container.

IMPORTANT TIP: Don't overcook!

Our Very Best Bar-B-Q Ribs

I must admit I didn't eat ribs very much until I left South Carolina. Ribs aren't a South Carolinian's idea of barbeque, so it took a little doin' to figure them out. Boy we had some fun practicing! Spare ribs have been replaced by leaner baby back ribs, and I recommend spending the extra money on the baby backs. They tend to be the least greasy. Country-style ribs tend to be too big and can be fatty. Stick with the baby backs.

SERVES 4.

> 1 bottle K.C. Masterpiece Barbecue Sauce
> ½ bottle Old El Paso (hot) Taco Sauce
> 1 tbsp. Worcestershire sauce
> 1 tbsp. soy sauce

1 tsp. garlic powder
Heavy sprinkle of red pepper flakes
4 slabs (4 to 5 lbs.) baby back ribs, cut in half

Start by making the sauce. Combine all ingredients except the ribs in a bowl. Stir well.

Line a large baking pan with aluminum foil. Place 4 half-slabs in baking pan, meaty side up. Baste with sauce. Place remaining slabs in pan and baste with sauce. Bake in a 350-degree oven for 30 minutes. Turn meaty side down, baste with sauce and bake for another 30 minutes. Turn meaty side up, baste and bake for another 30 minutes.

In the meantime, you need to prepare for finishing the ribs. This can be done under the broiler in the oven or on the grill. Under each option (I recommend the grill), cook till ribs are charred to your liking, turning only once.

Broiler

Remove ribs from baking pan and drain off drippings. Place rack in pan and place ribs on the rack. Baste with additional sauce and broil for a few minutes on each side.

Grill

Right after you put the ribs into the oven to bake, light your charcoal. If you're using a gas grill, pre-heat for 15 minutes before ribs come out of the oven. Use hickory chips (soaked in water for 30 minutes) if you want a smokier flavor. After the ribs are baked in the oven, baste them with additional sauce. Throw 'em on the grill and cook 5 to 10 minutes on each side. Watch for flare-ups or your ribs may be too charred. If that happens, wrap them carefully, pack in dry ice and send to Roy via Federal Express. He'll let you know if you've overdone it. Sorry, no returns.

Dry Rubbed Ribs

Some folks insist on rubbing their ribs. Sounded a little kinky to me, but I was willing to give it a try and we were pleasantly surprised. This approach entails rubbing the slabs with dry spices and seasonings before the cooking. The barbeque sauce is only

used very late in the process. Anyway, as long as it's pork and it's not overcooked, you can't miss!
SERVES 4.

> ¼ cup fresh ground black pepper
> ¼ cup granulated brown sugar
> ¼ cup paprika
> 1 tbsp. garlic powder
> 1 tsp. cayenne
> ½ tsp. Colman's dry mustard
> 4 slabs (4 to 5 lbs.) baby back ribs, cut in half

Combine all dry ingredients and blend well. Sprinkle on meat and rub in before cooking. Let ribs rest while the oven is preheating.

Place slabs, meat side up, in a large foil-lined baking pan and cook for 1½ hours in 300-degree oven or on your gas grill. Turn once about midway through cooking time.

Baste with barbeque sauce and use the same finishing process as for Our Very Best Bar-B-Q Ribs (p. 22).

Stuffed Pork Chops

Roy loves stuffed pork chops! At some butcher shops, you can buy them already stuffed, but I prefer to stuff my own. It isn't complicated and takes only a few extra minutes.
SERVES 4.

> 4 boneless butterfly loin chops
> Black pepper
> Garlic powder
> 2 tbsp. butter, margarine, or low-calorie substitute
> ¼ cup onion, chopped
> ¼ cup bell pepper, chopped
> ¼ cup mushrooms, chopped
> 1½ cups Easy Herb Stuffing Mix (p. 45)
> ¼ cup warm water
> Soy sauce

Pound pork chops with wooden mallet until they soften. (This will make them more malleable and easier to stuff.) Sprinkle with pepper and garlic powder and set aside.

Sauté onion and bell pepper in butter until tender, about 5 minutes. Add mushrooms and cook another 2 minutes.

In mixing bowl combine stuffing mix and sautéed vegetables. Blend well adding a little warm water at a time until the mixture is slightly pasty and begins to bind. Let cool.

Place pork chops on a platter and spoon about ½ cup of the stuffing mixture onto each. Fold the sides of the chops up toward the middle. Suture the chops with toothpicks. Insert the first toothpick about 1 inch from the top end, pulling the two sides close together. Place the second toothpick about one inch from the bottom end. The third toothpick should be placed in the middle. (The stuffing may ooze a little bit, but that's OK, there's plenty.) Sprinkle soy sauce on outside surface of pork chops.

Place on grill over medium heat "spine" side down. After 30 minutes, gently turn the chops on one side, then 10 minutes later turn to other side and cook for another 10 minutes. (This'll brown the chops without letting the stuffing fall out.)

Remove the toothpicks before serving. Roy almost ate one!

OPTION If you're pressed for time, substitute Pepperidge Farm Seasoned Stuffing for Easy Herb Stuffing Mix.

Dijon Pork Roast

Mustard is a natural enhancer for all cuts of pork. Most folks are used to tomato-based sauces, but tomato just doesn't bring out the best in a pork roast. Tomato-based sauces work well on ribs and chicken, but we prefer mustard on roasts and barbeque.
SERVES 4.

2½-lb. boneless pork roast
1 tsp. garlic powder with parsley
Salt and pepper to taste
3 tbsp. Dijon mustard
2 tbsp. flour

Rub roast with garlic powder with parsley, salt and pepper. Smear entire roast with mustard. Sift light covering of flour over roast.

Place on rack in pan and cook slowly in 325-degree oven until meat thermometer reaches 165 degrees, about 1½ hours.

Slice thin and serve immediately.

![decorative divider]

"Nawlins"-Style Pork Roast

I n addition to mustard, a few other spices add a little zest and ensure you'll be drinking a lot of iced tea with your dinner. I don't know if they even eat this in New Orleans, they're so busy with their crawfish and redfish, but I'm sure they would if they knew about it.
SERVES 4.

> 2½ lb. boneless pork roast
> 1 cup onions, chopped
> ½ cup garlic, chopped
> 2 tbsp. spicy, hot mustard
> 2 tbsp. Worcestershire sauce
> 2 tbsp. Horseradish Sauce (p. 61)
> 1 tbsp. Carolina Heat (p. 50)

Cut shallow slits across top of roast. In a mixing bowl, combine remaining ingredients and mix well. Stuff mixture into slits and spread remainder on top of roast.

Cook in 325-degree oven or over low heat on grill until meat thermometer reads 165 degrees. Let roast rest for 10 minutes before serving.

![decorative divider]

Momma's Sausage Pudding

M omma adapted a traditional Charleston cheese pudding recipe so it can be used as an entree. It's great for a brunch or even with barbeque.
SERVES 8.

> 1 lb. spicy, hot sage sausage
> 10 slices white bread, crust removed
> 3 tbsp. butter, softened
> 8 oz. sharp cheddar cheese, grated
> 2 cups milk
> ½ tsp. salt
> Pepper to taste
> 3 eggs, beaten

Crumble sausage into small pieces and cook in skillet over medium heat until brown. Drain well and cool slightly.

Butter slices of bread and cut into cubes. Place alternating layers of bread cubes and cheese into a 9 × 13-inch baking dish. Top with sausage.

Combine milk, salt, pepper and eggs. Mix well then pour over layers in baking dish. Let sit 3 to 4 hours before baking. Bake in 300-degree oven for 45 minutes.

■□■□■□■□■□■□■□■□■□■

Kyle's Romp in the Hay

My friend Kyle's favorite recipe has been eaten by hundreds of folks in the Washington, DC, area at some of her world-famous dinner parties. It was always amazing how many people could fit in her small apartment for those gala events. She and I spent most of our time in the kitchen together cooking, tasting and drinking just a little wine. We never burned a thing, but we've been known to take a nap between courses.

SERVES 6.

12 tbsp. butter
1 clove garlic, minced
2 lbs. hot Italian sausage, crumbled
1 tbsp. parsley, chopped
1 tsp. basil
¼ tsp. tarragon
¼ tsp. thyme
¼ tsp. oregano
¼ tsp. sage
¼ tsp. nutmeg
Salt and pepper to taste
2 lbs. mushrooms, sliced
1 lb. green ribbon noodles
1 lb. white ribbon noodles
1½ cups heavy cream
1 10-oz. box frozen peas, thawed
½ cup Parmesan cheese, grated
Freshly ground black pepper

Melt 10 tbsp. of the butter in large Dutch oven. Add garlic and cook until golden brown. Add sausage, parsley and other seasonings and cook for 20 minutes, stirring occasionally. Add mushrooms and cook 15 minutes, stirring occasionally. Keep hot.

Meanwhile, cook noodles according to package directions. Drain well, return to pot and add remaining 2 tbsp. butter. Sauté noodles over low heat. Add half of the sausage mixture and all the cream and the peas. Toss well over medium heat until cream thickens, about 3 minutes. Pour onto serving platter. Top with remaining sausage mixture and cheese. Grind a little fresh black pepper on top.

■■■■■■■■■■■■■■■■■■■

Italian Sausage Sauce

Since I didn't have enough pasta and sauce recipes for a separate chapter, I put this one in the pork chapter since Italian sausage is the meat of choice. I've also made it with ground round or a combination, but Roy prefers all Italian sausage. Maybe he thinks this is Italy's answer to barbeque. Serve over vermicelli or angel hair pasta with freshly grated Romano. This freezes well, so make a big batch when you have some extra time. SERVES 8.

3 lbs. hot Italian sausage
2 tbsp. olive oil

2 large onions, chopped
3 cloves garlic, minced
1 large bell pepper, chopped
1 lb. mushrooms, sliced
2 28-oz. cans crushed tomatoes
1 28-oz. can whole Italian tomatoes
2 6-oz. cans tomato paste
3 6-oz. cans water
2 tbsp. oregano
1 tbsp. basil
1 tbsp. parsley
1 tsp. thyme
1 tsp. granulated brown sugar
1 tsp. salt
Romano cheese, grated
2 bay leaves

Form sausage into small meatballs. In large skillet, brown sausage for 10 to 15 minutes, stirring frequently. Remove sausage and drain well. Place in 8-quart Dutch oven.

Heat olive oil and cook onions, garlic and bell pepper until tender. Add to Dutch oven. Combine remaining ingredients in Dutch oven and bring to a boil, reduce heat and simmer uncovered for at least 2 hours. The longer the better. Add additional water if sauce becomes too thick. Stir occasionally.

Cook your favorite pasta according to package directions. Drain well and toss with a little butter or margarine. Serve with Romano cheese.

■■□■□■□■□■□■□■□■□■□■□■

Heavenly Pig Pasta

You'll be in hog heaven when you taste this. SERVES 4.

1 lb. hot Italian sausage,
   crumbled
½ cup pine nuts, toasted
8 oz. fresh spinach
3 oz. sun-dried tomatoes
1 16-oz. pkg. angel hair pasta
1 tbsp. butter
½ cup light cream

½ cup Parmesan cheese, grated
Fresh ground black pepper

Brown sausage and drain well. Set aside. Place pine nuts on cookie sheet and bake in 350-degree oven until lightly toasted, about 5 minutes.

Blanch spinach and squeeze until dry. Blanch tomatoes and squeeze until dry. Set aside.

Cook pasta according to package directions. Drain well and return to pot. Over low heat add butter, cream and cheese. Toss until well blended and sauce thickens. Add sausage, spinach and tomatoes. Toss and serve immediately with extra cheese and fresh ground black pepper.

POULTRY

Chicken is a natural for preparation on a gas or charcoal grill. Many people have complained to me that they get unsatisfactory results, usually dry meat, so I have devoted some time to mastering the art of moist chicken on the grill. Actually you can even poach a chicken dry, so I cover that cooking technique in the "Salads" chapter.

The versatility of chicken can't be overstated! It's an excellent substitute for veal in many recipes. (Chicken Marsala is a good example.) It even substitutes well in many seafood recipes—Seafood Gumbo (p. 58) can readily become Chicken Gumbo. Pineapple Marinade, in the "Beef" chapter, works well for chicken too.

Momma's Chicken and Wild Rice

You'll dirty most every pot and pan in your kitchen making this dish, but the results are worth it. Just ask my momma! Just ask Roy! Make sure you have 3 pots, 2 bowls, 2 pans and a 2-quart casserole dish before you get started. You'll love the buttery aroma when the chicken's baking. It's irresistible! And it's perfect for a dinner party. Serve with a small green salad, steamed asparagus, warm crusty bread and a dry white wine. Freezes well. Reheats well.
SERVES 8.

6 lbs. chicken (2 whole chickens, or substitute thighs and breasts)
1 6-oz. pkg. Uncle Ben's long grain and wild rice mix
½ cup uncooked white rice
1 small bell pepper, chopped
1 tbsp. butter
½ lb. fresh mushrooms, sliced
1 can water chestnuts, sliced
2 cans cream of mushroom soup
1 cup milk
Salt and pepper to taste
2 sticks butter
4 cups Easy Herb Stuffing Mix (p. 45)

Pot #1—In large stockpot, cover chicken with water and bring to a boil. Reduce heat and simmer until tender and done, about 25 minutes. Don't overcook! Let cool slightly then bone and cut chicken into large bite-size pieces. (Save the chicken broth for other recipes. It'll keep in the freezer indefinitely.)

Bowl #1—Place chicken pieces into large mixing bowl.

Pot #2—Prepare wild rice according to package directions using ⅓ cup less water.

Pot # 3—Cook white rice (see Steamed Rice recipe [p. 79].)

Pan #1—Sauté bell pepper in 1 tbsp. butter until tender. Add wild rice, white rice, bell pepper, mushrooms, water chestnuts, cream of mushroom soup (undiluted) and milk to chicken in mixing bowl. Add salt and pepper to taste. Mix well.

Dish #1—Pour chicken mixture into large buttered casserole dish.

Pan #2—Melt the butter.

Bowl #2—In medium bowl, combine butter and herb dressing. Top casserole evenly with dressing mixture.

Bake uncovered in 350-degree oven for 30 minutes. (Count 'em! See, I told you you'd dirty every pot and pan you have!)

TIP An 8-oz. package of Pepperidge Farm Herb Seasoned Stuffing can be substituted for the Easy Herb Stuffing Mix.

TIP Don't bake the casserole if you plan to freeze it. If casserole has been frozen, thaw to room temperature before baking.

Cornish Game Hen on the Grill

This recipe is best prepared over charcoal with hickory chips, although a gas grill may be more convenient in the winter. If your dinner guests aren't big eaters like some folks we know, the game hens can be split in half. Serve with Rice Pilau (p. 80) or Hoppin' John (p. 81) and Charleston Squash Pie (p. 91). As long as you've got the grill going, Tomatoes on the Grill (p. 99) provide additional color.

SERVES 4 TO 8.

> *4 Cornish game hens, fresh or thawed*
> *1 cup vegetable oil*
> *1 cup red wine*
> *1 cup white wine*
> *3 tbsp. lemon juice*
> *3 tbsp. soy sauce*
> *3 tbsp. Worcestershire sauce*
> *1 tbsp. garlic, chopped*
> *1 small onion, chopped*

Combine all ingredients except hens and mix well. Place hens in nonmetallic pan and pour on marinade. Marinate for at least 4 hours, turning several times. (Can be marinated overnight in the refrigerator if you prefer.) Drain hens well before cooking and reserve marinade.

Soak hickory chips in water for 20 to 30 minutes. Place moist chips on hot charcoals just before putting hens on the grill. Baste hens every 20 minutes. If hens have been split, baste and turn every 10 minutes. Total cooking time: 50 to 60 minutes, depending on the intensity of the fire.

OPTION If you'd like some gravy for your rice, see Gravy from Marinade recipe on page 66.

■■■■□■□■□■□■□■□■□■■■■

Chicken on the Grill

There's nothing better tasting or better for you than chicken cooked on a grill. The secret to moist chicken is systematic and frequent basting and turning. The lemon garlic basting mixture serves as the basis for many chicken dishes and offers great variation. We like chicken with some type of rice—Red Rice, Lemon "Pealoff," Bama's Okra Purlow, Sherpa Rice (see "Rice" chapter, page 75), etc., and Zucchini on the Grill (p. 90).
SERVES 4.

2 split broilers (½ chicken per person), skinned

Lemon Garlic Baste

This basting mixture will help ensure moist, crispy chicken on the grill.

8 tbsp. butter or margarine (a low-calorie substitute is fine, too)
1 tbsp. lemon juice
1 tsp. garlic powder with parsley flakes
Pepper to taste

Combine basting ingredients in small saucepan and cook until margarine is melted. Cool slightly.

Lemon Garlic Chicken

Spoon some over chicken and let stand for 20 minutes before putting on the grill. Baste chicken with remainder and turn every 10 minutes. Total cooking time: 45 to 50 minutes, depending on the intensity of the fire.

Barbeque Chicken

Baste with Lemon Garlic and turn every 10 minutes. Baste chicken with barbeque sauce 10 minutes before end of cooking time. Turn once. Our favorite barbeque sauces for chicken are Boucanier from Greensboro, NC, and K.C. Masterpiece, spicy or hickory flavor. Or better yet, use your own secret recipe. My secret recipe, Carolina Gold, is on page 22.

Herb Chicken

Add 2 tbsp. of herbs from Provence (thyme, basil, savory, fennel, and lavender) to the Lemon Garlic ingredients. Sprinkle additional herbs on chicken before grilling.

Cajun Chicken

Add 2 tbsp. of Carolina Heat (p. 50) to the Lemon Garlic ingredients.

Hawaiian Chicken

Marinate chicken in 1 cup pineapple juice, 1 cup white wine and 1 tbsp. soy sauce for 2 to 4 hours before cooking. When grilling, baste chicken with marinade and turn every 10 to 15 minutes. Total cooking time: 45 to 50 minutes, depending on the intensity of the fire.

Greek Chicken

Modify Lemon Garlic ingredients. Substitute olive oil for 2 tbsp. margarine, increase garlic powder to 1 tbsp. and add 1 tbsp. oregano.

Hickory Chicken

Add ½ tsp. Liquid Smoke to the Lemon Garlic ingredients. Soak hickory chips in water for 20 to 30 minutes. Drain well. Place chips on hot coals in charcoal grill or in aluminum pan in preheated gas grill. When chips begin to smoke, put chicken on the grill. Baste and turn every 10 minutes. Total cooking time: 45 to 50 minutes, depending on the intensity of the fire.

Rosemary Chicken

Marinate chicken in 1 cup dry red wine, ½ cup Italian dressing (homemade, bottled or low-calorie), 1 tbsp. ketchup, 1 tsp. Worcestershire sauce, ½ tsp. rosemary and ½ tsp. marjoram for 2 to 4 hours before cooking. When grilling, baste chicken with marinade and turn every 10 to 15 minutes. Total cooking time: 45 to 50 minutes.

Mary's Special Chicken

This is a favorite recipe of a very good friend of mine and the inspiration for the title of the book. We used to prepare this one quite frequently when we were first learning our way around the kitchen together. "Cream of something" soup is sometimes an indication there's a beginner in the kitchen. It was in this case, but the recipe has staying power. It's still wonderful! It's great for an informal dinner party or a brunch, since it's considered "fork-ready" food. Once I cooked two batches for a dinner party with 16 guests. I planned to freeze the leftovers, but I had only about two bites left. Roy was the guest of honor. It's one of his favorites!

SERVES 12, UNLESS ROY'S INVITED.

8 whole chicken breasts, cooked and boned
1 can artichoke hearts, drained and quartered
1 can cream of mushroom soup
½ can milk
½ lb. fresh mushrooms, sliced
2 8-oz. cans water chestnuts, sliced
½ tsp. rosemary
½ tsp. oregano
½ tsp. onion salt
1 tsp. Worcestershire sauce
Pepper to taste
½ cup white wine
½ cup grated sharp cheddar cheese

Cut chicken into bite-size pieces. Mix all ingredients except wine and place into a 3-quart casserole dish. Bake uncovered in 350-degree oven for 20 minutes. Add wine, top with cheese and bake an additional 10 to 15 minutes.

Chicken Spoleto

Near the end of May, Charleston becomes the cultural focus of the world as the Spoleto Festival starts three weeks of wonderful entertainment—there's opera, jazz, ballet, art shows—throughout the city. Since the festival was started by an Italian, it seems only fitting that a chicken pasta dish should commemorate this festive time. Serve this with some warm crusty bread and a small Caesar salad. Then follow with something lemony for dessert.
SERVES 4.

4 tbsp. butter
4 tbsp. flour
2 cups milk, warmed
Pinch of nutmeg
Pinch of salt
Pinch of cayenne
2 whole chicken breasts, cooked, boned and
    shredded
½ lb. fresh mushrooms, sliced
1 lb. green ribbon noodles
Parmesan cheese, freshly grated

In top of double boiler, melt butter. Add flour and stir until well blended. Cook until roux is smooth and golden in color. Slowly add milk, stirring constantly until mixture thickens, about 15 minutes. Add spices. Add chicken and mushrooms to sauce. Simmer uncovered for 15 minutes. Adjust seasonings if needed.

Meanwhile, cook noodles according to package directions until tender. Drain well and place into warm serving bowl. Add half the chicken sauce mixture and toss well. Pour remaining sauce on top and serve immediately with freshly grated Parmesan cheese.

Chicken and Broccoli

The wok offers another opportunity for many healthful and low-calorie variations. While Charlestonians don't generally use woks, I don't think a cast-iron skillet would produce the same results. Omit the red peppers if you don't like hot foods or add more if you dare. Just be sure to remove all red peppers before serving. Keep vanilla ice cream on hand in case you miss one. It'll cool off your tongue quicker than you can say Jack Robinson. SERVES 6.

2 whole chicken breasts, boned and
    skinned
3 tbsp. soy sauce
1 tbsp. dry sherry
1 tsp. garlic powder
½ tsp. ground ginger
4 to 6 Chinese red hot peppers
1 cup boiling water
1 tsp. chicken bouillon granules
1 tbsp. lemon juice
1 tbsp. cornstarch
2 tbsp. benne (sesame) seeds,
    toasted
3 cups broccoli flowerets
1 small onion, sliced
1 small red bell pepper, sliced
1 cup fresh mushrooms, sliced
1 8-oz. can bamboo shoots
1 can rice noodles

Cut chicken into ¼-inch slices and marinate in soy sauce, sherry, garlic powder, ginger and hot peppers for 30 minutes or more.

Combine boiling water and bouillon granules in a measuring cup. Pour ½ cup of bouillon into another cup and add lemon juice and cornstarch. Blend well and set aside.

Heat wok to 300 degrees. Add benne seeds and stir fry for 1 minute. Seeds toast very quickly, so stir constantly. Remove toasted seeds from wok and set aside.

Increase heat to 375 degrees. Add remaining plain bouillon and broccoli to wok. Stir fry for 4 minutes. Push broccoli up the side of the wok. Add onion and bell pepper and cook for 1 minute. Add chicken and stir fry for 4 minutes. Push up the side again. Add mushrooms and bamboo shoots and stir fry for 1 minute. Mix all ingredients in the wok. Let simmer for 1 or 2 minutes.

Slowly add cornstarch mixture to the wok and cook until sauce thickens. Add benne seeds and serve with rice noodles.

TIP Be sure to remove all the hot peppers before serving. I missed one just once and, of course, Roy ate it. He still remembers and reminds me of it every time I use the wok.

■□■□■□■□■□■□■□■□■□■□■□■

Chicken What's-It-to-Ya

Ratatouille, or "What's It to Ya" as it's known in our house, is a wonderful vegetable dish that has been turned into an entree by using chicken. This tastes great hot or cold!
SERVES 6.

¼ cup olive oil
2 large onions, sliced
1 clove garlic, minced
1 lb. eggplant, peeled and cut into small cubes
¾ lb. zucchini, sliced
1 bell pepper, sliced
4 lbs. chicken (breasts and thighs)
2 tbsp. flour
½ cup water
1 28-oz. can tomatoes and liquid
1 lb. potatoes, cut into 1-inch cubes
1 tsp. fresh basil, chopped
1 tsp. fresh oregano, chopped
½ tsp. salt
½ tsp. sugar
¼ tsp. pepper

In a Dutch oven, cook onions and garlic in olive oil until golden brown, about 5 minutes over medium heat. Add eggplant, zucchini and bell pepper and cook for another 5 minutes. Stir constantly. Remove from pot and set aside.

Bone chicken and cut into serving-size pieces then add to pot and cook until browned. Stir in flour. Gradually add water and tomatoes with liquid from can. Add potatoes and seasonings. Bring to a boil, reduce heat, cover and simmer for 30 minutes. Add eggplant, zucchini and bell pepper and cook for another 5 minutes. Mix well. Cover, remove from heat and let stand for 10 minutes before serving.

Serve hot or cold.

Chicken Kabobs

This recipe is great for entertaining since so much can be done ahead and the cooking time is short. It can be cooked on the grill or under the broiler. Try hickory chips for a change if you cook over charcoal. Serve over Steamed Rice (p. 79) with a Tomato on the Grill (p. 99) as a garnish.
SERVES 6.

MARINADE

⅓ cup lemon juice
¼ cup vegetable oil
¼ cup white wine
1 tbsp. cider vinegar
1 tbsp. sugar
½ tsp. cayenne
1 clove garlic, minced

KABOBS

4 whole chicken breasts, boned, skinned and
  cut into bite-size pieces
¾ lb. zucchini, sliced into ½-inch pieces
½ lb. fresh mushrooms, halved

LEMON BUTTER

4 tbsp. butter, margarine or low-calorie
  substitute
1 tbsp. lemon juice
1 tbsp. parsley, chopped
Pepper to taste

Combine all marinade ingredients and pour over chicken in nonmetallic bowl. Marinate for at least 2 hours.

Combine all lemon butter ingredients in a small saucepan and cook over low heat until melted.

Prepare skewers, alternating chicken, zucchini and mushrooms. Baste with lemon butter and let stand for 15 minutes before cooking.

While cooking, baste and turn every 5 minutes. Total cooking time 12 to 15 minutes.

OPTION Chicken kabobs make great appetizers too! Use small bamboo skewers for cocktail-size kabobs. Place 2 to 3 pieces of chicken on each skewer with zucchini slices and parboiled pearl onions.

Momma's Southern Fried Chicken

Roy's favorite chicken is actually fried chicken, but he seldom has it at home since the caloric potential is astronomical. He'll eat it till he drops, so fried chicken is reserved for preparation by Momma and a few select restaurants throughout the Southeast. On our annual pilgrimage last summer, Roy ate fried chicken 8 times in 14 days. Pretty amazing! His two favorite restaurants for fried chicken are Michie Tavern in Charlottesville, VA, and the Smith House in Dahlonega, GA. Actually he likes Parker's in Wilson, NC, the Beaumont Inn in Harrodsburg, KY . . . well for that matter, as long as it's "all you can eat," he loves it.
SERVES 6.

3 to 4 lbs. chicken breasts, thighs, wings and
 legs
1 cup flour
1 tbsp. parsley, chopped fine
1 tsp. cayenne
1 tsp. black pepper
1 tsp. paprika
1 tsp. garlic powder
¼ tsp. salt
Vegetable oil, enough for frying

Remove skin from breasts, thighs and legs. Cut chicken breasts in half. (Smaller pieces cook faster and have less opportunity to dry out.) If the thighs are large, cut them in half too.

Combine dry ingredients and sift into small brown paper bag. Place a few chicken pieces at a time into the bag. Shake well to coat.

Deep Frying

Heat oil to 350 degrees in a deep fat fryer. Add 6 to 7 pieces chicken and cook until crisp and lightly browned, about 15 minutes. Drain on paper towels. Cook remaining chicken, 6 to 7 pieces at a time.

Pan Frying

Heat large frying pan to moderate temperature. Add enough vegetable oil to 2-inch depth in pan. Add chicken, cover and cook for 5 to 7 minutes. Turn chicken when the underside is golden brown. Cook for another 5 to 7 minutes. Reduce heat, cover and cook for another 20 to 25 minutes turning chicken only once.

Thanksgiving Turkey on the Grill

This isn't so tricky as you might think and the results will warrant the extra outdoors effort. Again, the secret is attention to the bird, not a lot of work. I recommend a Weber Genesis grill (it's easier) or a traditional Weber kettle. A covered grill is essential to ensure a moist bird. There's a difference of opinion about the merits of stuffing a bird, but I would opt for it. After all, Roy prefers it that way!

This recipe assumes a 14- to 16-pound turkey. SERVES 8 TO 10 (WITH LEFTOVERS FOR ROY).

STUFFING

8 cups *Easy Herb Stuffing Mix (p. 45) (or substitute 1 16-oz. package Pepperidge Farm Herb Seasoned Stuffing)*
2 tbsp. butter
1 cup onion, chopped fine
½ cup red bell pepper, chopped fine
½ cup green bell pepper, chopped fine
1 cup celery, chopped fine
1 lb. mushrooms, chopped
1 stick butter, melted
3 hard-boiled eggs, grated
2½ cups chicken stock

Pour stuffing mix into large mixing bowl.

Sauté onion, bell pepper and celery in 2 tbsp. butter until just tender. Add mushrooms and cook another minute.

Add sautéed vegetables, melted butter and eggs to bowl. Stir well. Slowly add half the stock. Mix well. Add remaining stock until consistency is moist, but not mushy. (You may use less than 2½ cups or need slightly more. This depends on the amount of moisture provided by the mushrooms, how well you measure, the relative humidity, etc.) Let stuffing mixture cool completely before you begin stuffing the bird.

Stuff body cavity loosely with stuffing. Sew or skewer opening shut. Then stuff neck cavity and secure neck skin under bird.

OPTION If you're willing to absorb a few extra calories, cook 1 lb. of pork sausage, drain well and combine with other stuffing ingredients. If you're Italian, use hot Italian sausage. If you're Polish, use kielbasa. If you're in Charleston, go to the Limehouse

Service Station at the foot of the westbound Ashley River bridge and get some famous Limehouse sausage.

Cooking the Bird

Place turkey breast side up in greased shallow pan. This is to ensure the sides brown evenly and you'll have easy access to all those wonderful drippings you'll need to make gravy.

Soak 2 cups of hickory chips in water for at least 20 minutes before cooking time.

Gas Grill Method—Preheat gas grill to 325 degrees. Place half the hickory chips into a disposable aluminum pan directly on flavorizer bars of the Weber Genesis or on lava rocks of other grills near a corner—or use a Weber Steam-N-Chips Smoker™ attachment. Once chips have begun to produce smoke, it's time for the turkey.

Charcoal Method—The indirect charcoal cooking method works very well for turkey. This keeps the bottom from burning and the juices from boiling away. If you have charcoal rails use them to keep your briquets to the side, otherwise place a large disposable aluminum pan in the middle of your coal rack and put briquets on each side.

When the coals are ready (ashen white), place half the hickory chips directly on the coals. They will produce smoke almost immediately. Add a few charcoal briquets to each side every hour. After about 2 hours, add the remaining hickory chips.

Both Grills—Place turkey in baking pan on the grill and close the lid. In about 20 minutes, go check on your bird. Take your bulb baster with you and start extracting those wonderful smoky juices from the pan. You'll just need to check in every 20 minutes or so to retrieve juices.

Baste the turkey with the pan juices a couple of times.

A stuffed bird should be done in 4½ to 5½ hours depending upon the vagaries of your grill. Refer to your poultry purveyor's instructions to determine doneness criteria.

TIP Monitor the bird's legs. When they move easily, it's probably done.

Smoky Turkey Gravy

The hickory smoke makes the nicest smoky gravy. You'll probably find yourself eating it by itself. So you'll diet until Easter, but you'll have a great Turkey Day! This freezes well, so make some extra to have with your leftovers. (We even have some turkey leftovers to freeze.)
MAKES ABOUT 2 CUPS.

¼ cup turkey fat drippings
¼ cup flour
2 cups pan juices and chicken stock
1 cup mushrooms, chopped
¼ cup skim milk
Salt and pepper to taste

Heat drippings in a saucepan over medium heat. Add flour and stir well until blended. Slowly add juices and stock. Cook until smooth, stirring constantly, then simmer for 5 minutes. Add mushrooms. Add half the milk very slowly. Stir constantly until you achieve a velvety consistency. Add remaining milk and cook 1 more minute.

Easy Herb Stuffing Mix

If you like to make stuffing from scratch, this is a quick no-fuss version. If you don't have time, buy some Pepperidge Farm Herb Seasoned Stuffing.
MAKES ABOUT 5 CUPS.

8 slices whole wheat bread
8 slices white bread
¼ cup parsley, chopped
1 tsp. sage
1 tsp. basil
1 tsp. black pepper, freshly ground

Spread slices of bread on cookie sheets. Bake in 200-degree oven for 20 minutes, turning once after 10 minutes. Allow bread to cool, remove crusts and discard. Dice bread. Toss in large bowl with spices.
   Store in airtight container in a cool, dry place.

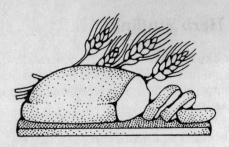

Flexible Bread Dressing

There are no exact proportions or ingredients for bread dressing except for a bread and spice base. Easy Herb Stuffing Mix serves as a jumping-off point into a dressing adventure. There are many possibilities. The Stuffing for Thanksgiving Turkey on the Grill (p. 43) is but one alternative.

Allow ½ cup of stuffing mix per person.

Use chicken stock and/or melted butter to moisten dressing mixture. If the mixture is too moist, add more stuffing mix. If it's too dry, add more stock or butter. Don't be afraid to experiment.

Use Flexible Bread Dressing to stuff chickens, game hens, pork chops or veal chops. Or, bake in shallow casserole in 350-degree oven for about 30 minutes and serve instead of rice or potatoes.

OPTIONAL INGREDIENTS Add what you'd like to Easy Herb Stuffing Mix.

Sautéed Vegetables—onions, green onions, shallots, celery, bell peppers (any color), mushrooms, carrots. Chop fine and sauté in butter until just tender.

Nuts and nut meats—pecans, pine nuts, almonds, water chestnuts, pistachios, walnuts. Chop larger nuts. Leave smaller nuts whole. Sauté in butter until coated.

Meats and seafoods—sausage, oysters, clams, shrimp. Brown sausage in skillet, break into small pieces and drain well. Chop oysters, shrimp, and clams then sauté in butter.

Other possibilities—chopped hard-boiled eggs, raisins or currants.

SEAFOOD

As you probably can guess from the number of recipes, we really love seafood. (Roy says, "See food and eat it.") I can't begin to say enough good things about seafood and the many opportunities it provides for dishes that'll make you think you've died and gone straight to Heaven. Most Charlestonians favor shellfish, but I've learned to cook a variety of fish as well.

Just like chicken, most seafood responds well to many spices and seasoning techniques. One fascinating aspect of seafood is how different varieties taste even when the identical spices or smoking woods are used. Each fish has distinctive flavor and texture. Cooking techniques that accentuate those characteristics are best.

Most shrimp recipes call for medium shrimp (30 to 36 shrimp per pound). The large and jumbo shrimp are best suited to grilling, stuffing and special fancy presentations. We prefer the medium shrimp as they tend to be "sweeter."

Crabmeat called for in the recipes is blue crab from the Atlantic and Chesapeake. There are other varieties—Alaskan king, snow, Dungeness, stone crab, etc.—but blue crab is the most delicate and flavorful. If you can't find it fresh, you probably can get pasteurized or frozen crabmeat. I don't recommend canned crabmeat.

There are many fish suitable for cooking on the grill—salmon, swordfish, halibut, grouper, tuna, mahi mahi, etc. You can produce professional results without a lot of fuss.

Two important points about seafood: Buy fresh and don't overcook!

Shrimp and Grits

This is Roy's favorite breakfast (or lunch or dinner) when we're in Charleston, or any place else for that matter. It's just that it tastes better in Charleston when Momma prepares it with sweet Carolina brown shrimp fresh from the shrimp trawlers. Yankees have even been known to eat this, although one of our neighbors left conspicuous "shrimp prints" in her grits. For dinner, serve with a small green salad and Aunt Mamie's Greek Corn Bread (p. 137). What an eclectic experience! For breakfast, serve with cheese biscuits.
SERVES 6, OR ROY.

    6 servings Quaker Oats Golden Grits, cooked
    ¾ cup sharp cheddar cheese, grated
    6 tbsp. butter
    3 lbs. medium shrimp, boiled, peeled and
        deveined
    3 tbsp. Carolina Heat (p. 50)

Cook grits according to package directions. When still slightly soupy, add cheese and 2 tbsp. butter. Stir well, remove from heat and cover to keep hot.

In a large skillet, sauté shrimp in 4 tbsp. butter and Carolina Heat until well coated and heated through, about 5 minutes. Once shrimp begin to brown slightly, they should be done. Don't overcook or they'll be tough.

Spoon grits into the center of each plate and allow to spread out. Place shrimp in the middle of the grits. Serve immediately.

TIP Don't overcook shrimp or they'll become tough and tasteless. Bring water to a boil in a large pot or Dutch oven. Add shrimp when water boils. Stir constantly. Reduce heat when water boils again. Total cooking time: 3 to 4 minutes. Rinse with cool water and drain in colander. Allow shrimp to cool before peeling and deveining.

Carolina Heat

I make this up in large batches. It'll keep for months in an airtight container. I usually make enough to give to neighbors and friends. We normally use it on seafood, but I've been known to sprinkle it on chicken and steaks, even scrambled eggs. MAKES ABOUT 2½ CUPS.

¾ cup paprika
5 tbsp. garlic powder
5 tbsp. onion powder
5 tbsp. cayenne
4 tbsp. black pepper, freshly ground
3 tbsp. white pepper, freshly ground
2 tbsp. thyme
2 tbsp. oregano

Combine all ingredients in large mixing bowl. Mix thoroughly.

Store in airtight container.

Spicy Shrimp Sauté

This is a quick dish sure to win rave reviews and requests for seconds. It was created one night when I discovered that my boss's wife didn't eat crabmeat. It was just before I was about to serve Deviled Crabs (p. 54) as the main course. I didn't panic (too much)! I opened the refrigerator and went to work while Roy entertained them. I grabbed a few of the boiled shrimp destined for Shrimp and Grits (p. 49) the next morning and a few vegetables. Minutes later, I was done, with no one the wiser. I suggest asking your guests if they eat shellfish before you plan your menu. Serve with Lemon "Pealoff" (p. 82) and tomato aspic. SERVES 4.

3 tbsp. butter
2 lbs. medium shrimp, boiled, peeled and deveined
1 small red bell pepper, diced
2 tbsp. green onion, chopped
2 tbsp. Carolina Heat (p. 50)
¼ lb. mushrooms, sliced thin

Melt butter in large sauté pan. Add shrimp, bell pepper, onions and Carolina Heat. Cook over medium heat stirring constantly for 3 to 4 minutes. Add mushrooms and cook an additional 2 minutes.

TIP Raw shrimp can be frozen and yet retain their fresh flavor with just a little special preparation. Buy fresh raw shrimp, rinse in cool water and place in plastic quart containers, leaving ½ inch free at the top. Fill container with water to cover shrimp. Wrap container in a plastic bag. Freeze immediately. To thaw, leave in refrigerator overnight or submerge container in warm water until thawed.

■■□■□■□■□■□■□■□■□■□■□■■

Lowcountry Shrimp

South Carolina is divided into two "countries"— the Lowcountry (that's us) and the Upcountry (that's them). Lowcountry residents eat a lot of seafood, love to entertain and drink on occasion. The Upcountry denizens don't like to dance or drink, but they love seafood too. You may not always be able to get a drink on Sunday in South Carolina, but you can always buy some seafood. This is no low-calorie dish! So serve with a simple green salad and steamed asparagus or broccoli. Serve over Holland rusk (Holland's cripsy version of English muffins, available at most gourmet shops), English muffins or Pepperidge Farm pastry puffs. Can be made a day ahead and refrigerated, but don't freeze.
SERVES 6.

> 6 tbsp. butter
> 6 tbsp. flour
> 1½ cups milk
> ¼ cup sherry
> Heavy pinch of mace
> Salt and pepper to taste
> 1½ lbs. medium shrimp, boiled, peeled and
>   deveined
> ½ lb. mushrooms, sliced
> 1 can quartered artichoke hearts, drained
> ¾ cup fresh Parmesan cheese, grated

In a heavy saucepan, melt butter, add flour and cook over medium heat until smooth and well blended. Add milk slowly and stir until sauce thickens. Remove from heat and add sherry, mace, salt and pepper. Add shrimp, mushrooms and artichoke hearts (drained). Pour mixture into buttered casserole and top with cheese. Cook uncovered in 375-degree oven until mixture bubbles, about 20 minutes. Don't overcook!

Carolina Shrimp Pilau

Shrimp and rice make a perfect combination as you'll soon see when you taste this dish. This is great for dinner when you're entertaining since the final preparation time is short and most of the work can be done ahead of time. Serve with Gazpacho Aspic (p. 117) and fresh asparagus. A nice dry white wine is a perfect companion and a lemony dessert is a refreshing finish.

SERVES 6.

4 slices bacon (see NOTE)
1½ cups long-grain white rice
1¼ cups water
1 tsp. Worcestershire sauce
2 lbs. medium shrimp, peeled and deveined
1 tbsp. flour
½ cup celery, chopped
½ cup red bell pepper, chopped
½ cup yellow bell pepper, chopped
3 tbsp. butter
4 to 5 drops Tabasco
Salt and pepper to taste

Fry bacon and set aside. Add bacon drippings to water for cooking the rice. Cook rice and keep warm (see Steamed Rice recipe on page 79).

Pour Worcestershire sauce on shrimp. Coat shrimp lightly with flour.

In large frying pan, sauté celery and bell pepper in butter until tender. Add shrimp and cook over medium heat until shrimp are pink and opaque, about 5 to 7 minutes. Add Tabasco, salt and pepper. Add cooked rice and bacon and mix well. Additional butter may be needed to ensure the dish is moist and buttery. Cover, remove from heat and give flavors a chance to blend for a few minutes. Don't worry—it's even good cold.

TIP Bacon and rice can be cooked earlier in the day. Chop celery and bell pepper and store in plastic bag. Peel and devein shrimp ahead and refrigerate until time to cook. Don't add Worcestershire and coat with flour until time to cook. With this much done ahead, the cooking time will be just a few minutes.

NOTE If bacon causes you dietary concern, reduce the number of slices to two. The flavor of bacon is essential to this dish, so it can't be omitted entirely.

■■■■■■■■■■■■■■■■■

Red Shrimp Pie

This "pie" has no crust, but is usually baked in a pie plate, hence the name. Momma suggests that you eat this in very, very low light. She doesn't like the appearance, but you can't beat the taste.
SERVES 6.

> 2 lbs. medium shrimp, boiled, peeled and
>   deveined
> 2 cups seasoned bread crumbs
> 2 cups tomato juice
> 1 cup ketchup
> 3 tbsp. butter
> 2 tbsp. Worcestershire sauce

> 1 tbsp. dried parsley
> 1 tsp. Tabasco sauce
> ½ tsp. salt

Combine all ingredients. Mix well and place into buttered casserole. Bake uncovered in 350-degree oven for 30 minutes.

■■■■■■■■■■■■■■■■■

White Shrimp Pie

Shrimp pie has almost as many variations as there are opinions about politics, religion or barbeque in Charleston. The "red vs. white" question has the potential of becoming as controversial as that surrounding clam chowder preferences. You have both recipes, so have a few friends over for a cook off and y'all decide!
SERVES 6.

> 2 lbs. medium shrimp, boiled, peeled and
>   deveined
> 2 cups seasoned bread crumbs
> 1 cup milk

2 tbsp. butter
2 tbsp. sherry
1 tbsp. dried parsley
1 tbsp. Worcestershire sauce
Salt and pepper to taste
Dash of mace

Combine all ingredients. Mix well and place into buttered casserole. Bake uncovered in 350-degree oven for 30 minutes.

■□■□■□■□■□■□■□■□■□■

Deviled Crabs

These little devils can be downright addictive! It's nice to use real crab shells, but since they're hard to come by, you can use small scallop baking shells. Make several batches at one time. They freeze well. You'll love heating these up one night when you really don't feel like cooking.
SERVES 6.

8 tbsp. butter, melted
¾ cup bread crumbs
2 tbsp. sherry
1 tbsp. Hellmann's mayonnaise
1 tsp. Worcestershire sauce
1 tsp. lemon juice
½ tsp. Colman's dry mustard
½ tsp. parsley
Salt and pepper to taste
1 lb. white crabmeat, picked twice for shell particles

Mix 4 tbsp. melted butter into ½ cup bread crumbs. Add sherry, mayonnaise, Worcestershire, lemon juice and other seasonings. Gently mix in crab to keep pieces from breaking up. Fill 6 shells with crab mixture. Sprinkle with bread crumbs. Melt remaining butter and pour on top.

Bake on an ungreased cookie sheet in 400-degree oven for 30 minutes.

TIP Be sure to pick the crabmeat at least twice. If you have family or friends like Roy, they are lightning rods for shells, particles and fish bones. It's uncanny! Sometimes I'll pick through the meat three times and Roy still finds something in his serving(s).

Meeting Street Crab

This is the very first recipe I ever prepared from *Charleston Receipts*. (That cookbook is an absolute must for your kitchen.) This is no low-calorie dish! The crab has a very rich taste, so serve with a small green salad and steamed asparagus or broccoli. Serve over Holland rusk, English muffins or toast points. Can be made a day ahead and refrigerated, but don't freeze.
SERVES 4.

4 tbsp. butter
4 tbsp. flour
1 cup Half & Half
4 tbsp. sherry
Salt and pepper to taste
1 lb. white crabmeat, picked twice for shell particles
¾ cup sharp cheddar cheese, grated

Make a white sauce with butter, flour and Half & Half. (Melt butter, add flour and cook over medium heat until smooth. Add Half & Half slowly and stir until sauce thickens.) Remove from heat and add sherry, salt and pepper. Add crab. Pour mixture into buttered casserole and top with cheese. Cook uncovered in 375-degree oven until mixture bubbles, about 20 minutes. Don't overcook!

TIP This makes great hot hors d'oeuvres. Serve in a chafing dish or fondue pot with small patty shells.

Carolina Crab Cakes

This dish is indigenous to the Chesapeake Bay area. I don't remember eating crab cakes as a child, but I certainly learned as an adult. Maryland-style crab cakes are a true delicacy. This recipe is a

South Carolina adaptation of the Maryland approach. They freeze well.

SERVES 4 (A MERE APPETIZER FOR ROY).

> 1 lb. lump crabmeat, picked at least twice for
>   shell particles
> 1/3 cup seasoned bread crumbs
> 2 eggs, beaten
> 2 tbsp. red bell pepper, diced
> 1 tbsp. green bell pepper, diced
> 1 tbsp. parsley, chopped fine
> 1/4 tsp. cayenne
> 1/4 tsp. Colman's dry mustard
> Heavy pinch of mace
> 2 tbsp. Hellmann's mayonnaise
> 3 tbsp. butter

Combine all ingredients except butter in large mixing bowl. Mix gently so crabmeat doesn't break up.

Refrigerate mixture at least 30 minutes to allow ingredients to bind.

Shape 8 crab cakes from the mixture. Pan fry in butter over medium heat until golden brown and crusty, about 2 minutes on each side.

Scallops "Scallopini"

After cooking Veal Scallopini Marsala several times, I decided to experiment with seafood and go for a really colorful dish. The flavors need to meld, so remove from heat, cover and let this sit for just a few minutes before serving. Serve with Steamed Rice (p. 79), steamed broccoli or asparagus and a nice green salad. We like Gingerbread Squares (p. 148) for dessert.

SERVES 4 (ROY ENDS UP HALF FULL AND I DON'T GET TO EAT).

> 1½ lbs. bay scallops
> 1 tbsp. flour
> Salt and pepper to taste
> 3 tbsp. butter
> 1 tbsp. olive oil
> 1/4 cup green bell pepper, sliced into strips
> 1/4 cup red bell pepper, sliced into strips
> 1/4 cup yellow bell pepper, sliced into strips
> 2 tbsp. green onion, sliced
> 1 lb. mushrooms, sliced
> 1/2 cup Marsala wine
> 1 tbsp. fresh parsley, chopped

Coat scallops with flour and spices. Heat a large skillet, then add 2 tablespoons butter and olive oil. Sauté scallops until lightly browned, about 3 minutes, stirring constantly. Remove from pan.

Sauté pepper slices in the remaining butter for 3 minutes. (It may be necessary to add some more butter.) Add onions and mushrooms, stir and cook another minute. Reduce heat, add wine and return scallops to pan. Cook until mixture becomes well blended. Stir in parsley and cook another minute. Remove from heat, cover and let sit for a few minutes before serving.

3 tbsp. butter
1 tbsp. lemon juice
1 tbsp. Worcestershire sauce
2 tbsp. onion, chopped
1 tsp. garlic powder
1 tsp. dried parsley
1 lb. salmon fillets or 2 salmon steaks
½ lb. fresh mushrooms, sliced

Combine butter, lemon juice, Worcestershire, onion, garlic and parsley in small saucepan and simmer until onion is tender and transparent. Let mixture cool slightly. Spoon half of sauce over salmon, reserving the other half, and let salmon marinate for 20 to 30 minutes.

Add mushrooms to reserved mixture and stir well to coat.

Place salmon, skin-side down for fillets, directly on the grill. Cook 10 to 12 minutes. Don't turn! Meanwhile, heat mushroom mixture. Spoon over salmon before serving.

OPTION Salmon cooked over hickory chips is simply the best thing you'll ever eat.

Salmon on the Grill

Salmon is a delicious fish no matter how it's prepared. Since salmon has a high fish-oil content, it can be grilled without drying out. This quick, easy recipe requires little effort as this flavorful fish does all the work.

SERVES 2 (DOUBLES OR TRIPLES EASILY).

Blackened Salmon

Chef Willie of Sunset Foods and I had a slight difference of opinion over the issue of blackening salmon. I think it's just wonderful; he says in his native language, *"C'est barbarique!"* I found out how he felt one day when I asked him to skin a salmon fillet for me and so did half the store. He's a wonderful high-spirited French Canadian who loves to cook. Anyway, despite Willie's rather loud protests, salmon is wonderful when it's blackened. Since this is rather spicy, you'll want to serve with vegetables that offset the heat. We like Yellow Squash Boats (p. 92) and Creamed Spinach (p. 96). SERVES 2.

    3 tbsp. butter
    1 lb. salmon fillet, skinned and cut into 2
       pieces
    2 tbsp. Carolina Heat (p. 50)

Melt butter and allow to cool slightly. Dip fillet pieces into butter, allow excess to drip off, then sprinkle both sides of fillets with Carolina Heat and gently rub in spices.

In cast iron skillet heated to at least 500 degrees, place fillets and top each with 1 tsp. of melted butter. Cook 2 minutes. Turn fillets, top each with 1 tsp. butter and cook for another 2 minutes. Serve immediately.

TIP Don't attempt this indoors unless you have an extremely powerful exhaust fan or you need an excuse to redecorate your kitchen or even your whole house. Since this cooking technique can be messy, I suggest you do it outside on a gas grill. It'll drive the neighbors crazy!

■■■■■■■■■■■■■■■

Seafood Gumbo

Gumbo is probably the third most popular Southern food art form after barbeque and fried chicken. The preparation of gumbo is steeped in Southern history and tradition. Most Southerners have a favorite family gumbo recipe. The word gumbo was derived from an African word for okra. Okra is a long, funny-looking, fuzzy green vegetable you've probably seen in your neighborhood market. Its taste is truly unique, so you'll have to experience it for yourself. Okra is used to thicken gumbo. Until recently, okra wasn't available year-round, so the folks in Louisiana somehow figured they could substitute filé (ground sassafras leaves) to thicken the gumbo. Filé adds a distinctive taste. It can overpower, so use it sparingly. We like to use both okra and filé. Seafood Gumbo will make you faint!! That's about all I can say about this recipe. It takes a little time, so make it on the weekend. It can be frozen, but I usually don't have any leftovers—remember Roy. SERVES 8.

½ cup flour
¼ cup oil
4 slices bacon
2 cups okra, sliced (preferably fresh)
2 onions, chopped and divided
½ cup bell pepper, chopped
½ cup green onion, chopped
½ cup parsley, chopped
1 28-oz. can tomatoes
2 qts. water
2 tbsp. Worcestershire sauce
1 tbsp. Tabasco sauce
1 tbsp. garlic, minced
1 tsp. salt
2 lbs. shrimp, peeled and deveined
1 lb. fish fillets, cut into pieces (use swordfish, grouper, halibut, monkfish or some other mild fish with firm flesh)
1 lb. bay scallops
4 cups Steamed Rice (p. 79)

Make a roux with the flour and oil in a large Dutch oven. (This should take about an hour until the roux develops a rich peanut butter color. Remember to stir constantly.) Set aside. Meanwhile, cook bacon, remove from frying pan and set aside. Then cook okra and half the onions in the bacon drippings until moisture is cooked out of the okra, about 20 minutes.

Add remaining onion and bell pepper to finished roux. Cook until onion becomes transparent. Add green onion, parsley, tomatoes, water, Worcestershire, Tabasco, garlic and salt. Add okra mixture. Cover and cook for 30 minutes. Add seafood and bacon. Simmer on low heat for another 1 to 1½ hours.

Serve piping hot over Steamed Rice. Add a little gumbo filé to individual servings for a decidedly different taste.

Scalloped Oysters

If you like oysters, you'll love this easy recipe. Serve over toast points with Glorified Grits (p. 84) and Stewed Tomatoes (p. 99). That'll warm you up on a cold winter night.
SERVES 6.

    1 quart fresh oysters
    ½ tsp. salt
    ½ tsp. pepper
    Dash of mace
    1 cup milk
    1 stick butter, melted
    1½ cups cracker crumbs

Drain oysters and reserve oyster liquor ("oyster juice"). Add liquor, salt, pepper and mace to milk in a small saucepan. Cover and place over low heat to gradually warm.

Combine melted butter and cracker crumbs. Grease casserole dish and alternate layers of crumbs and oysters, crumbs first. (You should have 3 layers of crumbs and 2 layers of oysters.) Pour 2 cups liquor and milk mixture over layers. Let stand at least 20 minutes before cooking. Bake at 375 degrees for 45 minutes.

Golden Fried Oysters

Generally I don't prepare fried foods. Oysters are great raw, steamed wet or dry, Rockefellered, scalloped, etc. At least once a year, however, I make an exception for oysters. Golden fried, served piping hot with very cold beer is a real treat! Roy likes Southern Fried New Potatoes (p. 94) and cole slaw with his fried oysters.
SERVES 4.

    2 eggs, beaten
    2 tbsp. milk
    1 tsp. garlic powder

½ tsp. cayenne
½ tsp. parsley, chopped
Salt to taste
1 quart select oysters, drained
1 cup seasoned bread crumbs
1 cup vegetable oil

Combine eggs, milk and seasonings. Dip oysters into egg mixture, then bread with seasoned crumbs.

Heat oil to moderate heat (375 degrees) in large frying pan. Cook oysters about 2 minutes on first side and then 1 minute on the other. Serve immediately with lemon wedges and Cocktail and Horseradish sauces (see below).

OPTION If you can find small select oysters, this makes a great appetizer.

Cocktail Sauce

Cocktail sauce is used as a foil for seafood. It's not meant to mask the taste, so don't overdo it.
MAKES 1 CUP.

1 cup ketchup
2 tbsp. horseradish
2 tbsp. lemon juice
1 tbsp. Worcestershire sauce
½ tsp. cayenne

Mix all ingredients and chill.

Horseradish Sauce

Even though I've included this recipe in the "Seafood" section, this sauce is wonderful with pork, roast beef or just about anything you want to spice up a little bit. Roy says it'll even cure the common cold.
MAKES 1 CUP.

¾ cup Hellmann's mayonnaise
⅓ cup lemon juice
¼ cup fresh parsley, chopped
4 tbsp. horseradish
1 tbsp. Worcestershire sauce
Salt and pepper to taste

Mix all ingredients and chill.

Fried Soft Shell Crabs

This can be done without ever touching the crabs if you didn't enjoy Biology lab in high school. Just have your seafood purveyor "clean" the crabs for you and buy a good pair of tongs. I guess rubber gloves could be used, but I prefer the tongs. Roy will eat all I cook, so it's useless to try to figure how many this will serve. So I'll assume I'm cooking a nice Sunday "lunch" for Roy. Serve with Bama's Okra Purlow (p. 81), Charleston Squash Pie (p. 91) and a little Mrs. Sassard's artichoke relish.
SERVES ROY.

3 tbsp. butter
1 tbsp. Carolina Heat (p. 50)
4 soft shell crabs, cleaned
½ cup seasoned bread crumbs

Melt butter in large frying pan, add spice and cool slightly. Dip crabs in butter and then dredge in bread crumbs. Reheat butter and cook crabs over moderate heat for 2 minutes on each side until golden brown.

OPTION Some people prefer an egg wash, so instead of using melted butter, use 1 egg, beaten, and ¼ cup milk.

BEEF AND VEAL

Beef loves to be marinated. And there are a lot of low-calorie marinade alternatives. Marinated beef tastes better, is more tender and gives a more predictable result. Besides you'll have the makings of some wonderful gravies in case you have some leftover rice.

Veal is a wonderfully delicate food that readily absorbs flavors. But it does require some physical exercise. No matter how lean and expensive the cut of veal, you'll still need your wooden mallet to flatten the meat. It's well worth the effort, since there's nothing better than paper-thin pieces of veal in a luscious sauce.

Beef Marinades

Roy is a great advocate of marinades, secret sauces as he calls them. These versatile marinades can be used for steaks, kabobs, London broil, sirloin tip roast, tenderloin, etc. The longer a piece of meat marinates the better, so I recommend at least 8 hours in the marinade under refrigeration or 2 hours at room temperature. If you want to cook a less expensive cut—flank steak, round steak, etc.—marinate under refrigeration for 24 to 48 hours.

- Allow ½ lb. of beef per person.
- Always use a nonmetallic dish or bowl.
- Cover with aluminum or plastic wrap.
- If meat has been frozen, thaw before marinating.
- Trim excess fat from meat.
- Turn meat several times as it marinates.
- Reserve marinade to make gravy.

Your own secret sauces can be developed with a little experimentation. So don't hesitate to be imaginative. These marinade recipes should give you a good start.

Pineapple Marinade

This is Roy's favorite marinade. It's especially good for London broil and tenderloin. Pineapple beef kabobs are tasty and the marinade makes luscious gravy for the rice.
SERVES 4.

1 6-oz. can unsweetened pineapple juice
1 cup dry red wine
¼ cup onion, sliced
1 tbsp. garlic powder
1 tbsp. Worcestershire sauce
1 tbsp. soy sauce
1 tsp. Kitchen Bouquet
1 tsp. black pepper
2 lbs. beef (tenderloin, steaks, London broil, sirloin tip roast, etc.)

Mix all marinade ingredients. Place meat into nonmetallic bowl or pan. Cover with marinade. Marinate at least 8 hours under refrigeration or 2 hours at room temperature. Baste and turn at least 3 times. Cook meat at 350 degrees until meat thermometer registers 140 degrees (rare) or better yet, cook it on the grill.

OPTION Tenderloin marinated in this pineapple concoction makes a great hors d'oeuvre too. Cook tenderloin until medium rare, slice thin and serve on small pumpernickel and rye rolls with horseradish sauce and Dijon mustard.

Italian Marinade

I like to use this marinade for London broil. It tákes the tenderizing effect of the red wine very well, but still has a nice chewy consistency. Serve with a green salad and Zucchini Matchsticks (p. 90) or steamed patty pan squash.
SERVES 4.

> 1 bottle Italian dressing
> 1 cup dry red wine
> 1 small onion, minced
> 1 tbsp. oregano
> 1 tbsp. dried parsley
> 1 tsp. black pepper
> 1 tsp. garlic powder
> 2 lbs. London broil or other beef

Combine all marinade ingredients. Pour over meat in nonmetallic bowl. Marinate in refrigerator for at least 8 hours. Cook meat in 350-degree oven until meat thermometer registers 140 degrees (rare) or better yet, throw it on the grill.

NOTE A low-calorie Italian dressing will work well, too.

Gravy from Marinade

This is great when you decide to splurge and serve rice or potatoes as an accompaniment. This gravy recipe works with any beef marinade, but it's especially good when Pineapple Marinade (p. 65) is used. The onions'll be so good you'll wish you'd used more than the recipe called for, so next time, experiment!
MAKES ABOUT 1½ CUPS.

> 1¼ cup Pineapple or Italian Marinade
> ¼ cup red or white table wine
> ½ lb. mushrooms, sliced
> 1 tbsp. cornstarch

Heat 1 cup of marinade and wine in saucepan. Add mushrooms and simmer over low heat for a few minutes.

In separate bowl, combine 3 tbsp. of marinade

with cornstarch and mix until smooth. Add slowly to marinade in pan, stirring until the mixture thickens.

Beef on the Grill

There's nothing better than a good steak cooked on the grill. There are a few techniques that can ensure a quality result each time. I highly recommend "smoking" beef on the grill. My first recollection of that wonderful hickory-smoked taste is owed to my friend Nancy's father. He would cook the most tremendous sirloin steaks I've ever tasted. He used virtually no seasonings, just a dash of seasoned salt and black pepper, a covered grill with a very hot fire and hickory chips. When I knew he was going to cook steaks, I always found an excuse to stay so I'd be invited to eat. And if I was home and the wind was out of the East, I'd find an excuse to go over to Nancy's. Few things in life smell as good as a big sirloin steak cooking over hickory chips!

A covered cooker such as a Weber kettle or Genesis grill really keeps the moisture in the beef. You'll be able to really char the outside of the steaks without sacrificing the juices. It's almost impossible to smoke without a covered grill. All the aroma goes up in smoke. (I couldn't resist.)

I recommend omitting salt, even seasoned salt. Use a marinade to provide additional flavor if you'd like. The soy sauce in marinades will give you that salty flavor. The Pineapple Marinade (p. 65) and hickory chips are our favorite combination for any kind of beef—kabobs, London broil, sirloin tip and top of round roasts, tenderloin, etc. It even makes burgers taste wonderful!

½ lb. steak per person
Marinade of your choice
Pepper to taste
2 cups hickory chips, soaked in water for 30
  minutes

When coals are ashen-gray, cover with wet hickory chips. Place steak on grill, cover and cook to desired doneness. Medium rare should take about 4 minutes on each side.

Stuffed Tenderloin of Beef

I love stuffed tenderloin for a festive occasion like our Christmas dinner. It's colorful and delicious. It's good hot or cold and makes a great leftover, that is if there's any left after dinner. If you want leftovers, don't invite Roy for tenderloin. SERVES 8.

1 whole beef tenderloin, trimmed (3 to 4 lbs.)
1 tbsp. black pepper
1 tsp. garlic powder
1 tbsp. Worcestershire sauce
3 tbsp. butter
1 cup green onions, sliced thin
1 clove garlic, diced
1 large red bell pepper, diced
1 large green bell pepper, diced
½ lb. white button mushrooms, sliced
½ lb. brown mushrooms, sliced
4 slices bacon (can be omitted)

Trim excess fat, if any, from tenderloin. Butterfly tenderloin by cutting lengthwise to within ½ inch of opposite side. Do not cut through opposite side.

Spread tenderloin open like a book. Tenderloin should lie flat. Mix pepper and garlic powder. Rub pepper and garlic on open surface of tenderloin, sprinkle on Worcestershire sauce and set aside.

Prepare stuffing mixture as follows: Sauté onions, garlic and bell peppers in butter until tender. Add mushrooms and cook another 2 minutes. Remove stuffing from heat and let cool slightly.

Spoon stuffing into opening of tenderloin. Fold top over stuffing. Tie tenderloin with heavy string every 2 to 3 inches to secure stuffing. Drape bacon slices over the top of the tenderloin. Place tenderloin on rack in roasting pan and bake in 425-degree oven until meat thermometer registers 140 degrees (rare) or 160 degrees (medium), about 20 to 30 minutes.

Let cool for 10 minutes before carving.

Blackened Steaks

Blackened steaks are almost as good as blackened salmon, but they're a lot easier to come by. Again, this is definitely an outdoors recipe, producing a lot of smoke and good smells. The suggested cooking time produces "medium" results, so adjust your cooking time to suit your preference. Roy likes these spicy steaks with Southern Fried New Potatoes (p. 94) and Creamed Spinach (p. 96). SERVES 4.

4 8-oz. rib-eye steaks, about ¾-inch thick
4 tbsp. butter, melted
3 tbsp. Carolina Heat (p. 50)

Dip steaks into butter, allow excess to drip off, then sprinkle with Carolina Heat, working spices into the surface. Into cast iron skillet heated to 500 degrees, place steaks and top each with 2 tsp. of melted butter. Cook 2 minutes. Turn steaks, add 1 tsp. butter on each and cook for another minute.

OPTION This works great with boneless pork chops too! Pound pork chops with wooden mallet until they're about ½-inch thick. Increase cooking time to 3 minutes on one side and 2 minutes on the other.

Steak Salad

This is quick, healthful and great for a summer supper. It'll satisfy a craving for red meat, while sneaking in a few tasty veggies. The steak is good hot or cold, but Roy likes his hot! SERVES 4.

1 tbsp. soy sauce
1 tsp. Worcestershire sauce
1 tsp. garlic powder
1 tsp. black pepper
1 lb. rib-eye steaks
1 head romaine lettuce
1 can artichoke hearts, quartered
1 yellow bell pepper, sliced
1 bunch green onions, sliced
12 cherry tomatoes, halved

12 ripe olives, sliced
Vinaigrette Dressing (p. 120) or prepared
ranch dressing

Combine sauces and spices. Pour over steaks, turning frequently to coat both sides. While steaks marinate, prepare vegetable components.

Tear romaine into large bite-size pieces and cover dinner plates with fluffy base of lettuce. Divide remaining ingredients evenly and place on lettuce base in symmetrical pattern. (Express your artistic talents!)

Cook steaks to medium doneness (panfry, broil or grill). Slice very thin and add to salad fixings. Top with a large dollop of dressing.

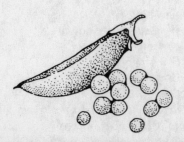

Beef and Pea Pods

Beef is well suited for wok cooking. I recommend the wok technique especially when you're not exactly sure when you're going to eat. Roy will be starved at 5:30 some days and may not want to eat until 9:00 the next night (but he always wants to eat), so this approach gives me a lot of flexibility. Prepare your ingredients ahead, put into plastic bags and refrigerate till you're ready. Then you're only 10 minutes away from the table. The longer the meat marinates, the tastier and more tender it'll be. SERVES 4.

1 lb. sirloin tip or round steak, cut into slices,
2-inches long by ¼-inch thick
3 tbsp. soy sauce
1 tbsp. vegetable oil
1 tbsp. dry sherry
1 tsp. garlic powder
½ tsp. ground ginger
6 red hot peppers (or more if you're up to it)
2 tbsp. vegetable oil
1 bunch green onions, sliced into ¼-inch
pieces; separate white parts from green parts

1 small red bell pepper, sliced into thin strips
1 cup beef bouillon, divided
1 cup pea pods
1 cup fresh mushrooms, sliced
1 8-oz. can water chestnuts, sliced and drained
1 tbsp. cornstarch
2 tbsp. benne (sesame) seeds, toasted
1 can rice noodles

Cut beef into slices and marinate in next 6 ingredients for at least 30 minutes.

Heat wok to 375 degrees. Add oil. Stir fry white parts of the green onions for 2 minutes. Push up the side of the wok. Stir fry bell pepper for 1 minute and push up the side. Stir fry beef 3 minutes. Push up the side. Add ½ cup bouillon to wok. Add pea pods, mushrooms, water chestnuts and green parts of the green onions. Stir fry for 2 minutes. Blend all ingredients in the wok. Combine remaining ½ cup bouillon and cornstarch. Stir slowly into the wok mixture and cook until sauce thickens. Add benne seeds and serve over rice noodles.

Veal, Mushrooms and Bell Peppers

This recipe really showcases the wonderful taste of veal. Marsala, while a very strongly flavored wine, does not overpower the delicate veal. The flavors need to fully develop, so let this sit for just a few minutes before serving. Serve over rice or noodles if calories aren't an issue, otherwise steamed asparagus and a salad would do just fine.
SERVES 4.

1½ lbs. veal scallops
3 tbsp. flour
Salt and pepper to taste
3 tbsp. butter
1 tbsp. olive oil
½ cup red bell pepper, sliced thin
¼ cup green onions, sliced
1 lb. mushrooms, sliced
½ cup Marsala wine
1 tbsp. fresh parsley, chopped

Pound veal with wooden mallet until ⅛-inch thick. Cut veal into serving-size pieces and coat with flour and spices. Heat large frying pan and add 2 tbsp. butter and olive oil. Sauté veal until lightly browned, about 3 to 4 minutes on each side. Remove from pan.

Sauté peppers and onions in the remaining butter for 2 minutes. (It may be necessary to add some more butter.) Add mushrooms, stir and cook another minute. Reduce heat, add wine and return veal to pan. Cook until mixture becomes well blended. Stir in parsley and cook another minute. Remove from heat, cover and let sit for a few minutes before serving.

■■■■■■■■■■■■■

Stuffed Veal Chops on the Grill

An easy delicious grill experience awaits you. Just be sure to buy thick veal chops, at least 1½-inches thick. Each chop should be 6 to 8 oz. or a little larger if someone of Roy's culinary persuasion is invited.

SERVES 4 (REGULAR FOLKS).

4 thick veal chops
Garlic powder
Salt and pepper to taste

MARINADE
   ½ cup vegetable oil
   1 cup dry white wine
   1 tbsp. rosemary
   1 tsp. thyme

STUFFING
   1 cup cooked white rice
   ½ cup cooked wild rice
   3 tbsp. butter
   ¼ cup carrots, chopped
   ¼ cup green onions, chopped
   ¼ cup currants

Place chops into shallow glass dish. Sprinkle spices over chops. In a jar, combine marinade ingredients. Mix well and pour over chops. Marinate several hours at room temperature or overnight in the refrigerator. Turn chops a few times while they marinate.

Meanwhile, prepare stuffing mixture. Cook rice

according to your method of preference. (See Steamed Rice [p. 79].) Place cooked rice into large bowl and keep warm. Sauté carrots and green onions in butter until tender but crisp. Add vegetables and currants to rice and mix well.

Remove chops from marinade and drain well. Cut pocket in each chop. Stuff each chop with rice mixture. Secure with toothpicks.

Cook on grill for 6 to 8 minutes on each side. A little longer if you like yours well done.

■■■■■■■■■■■■■■■■

Benne Veal Scallops

T his veal recipe has all the ingredients we hold dear—tender veal scallops, benne seeds, a lemony sauce and a little white wine. This dish is usually reserved for company. Serve with steamed asparagus, Southern Fried New Potatoes (p. 94) and a grilled tomato for color. Start with Seafood Gumbo (p. 58) and finish with Blueberries Jubilee (p. 146).

And don't forget a nice Chardonnay or Fumé Blanc. I think you can skip the bread this time.
SERVES 6.

2 lbs. veal scallops
3 tbsp. flour
¼ tsp. garlic powder
Salt and pepper to taste
4 tbsp. butter
Juice of 1 lemon
¼ cup dry white wine
2 tbsp. fresh parsley, chopped
2 tbsp. benne seeds, toasted

Pound veal with wooden mallet until ⅛-inch thick. Cut veal into serving-size pieces and coat with flour and spices. Heat large skillet and add butter. Sauté veal until lightly browned, about 3 to 4 minutes on each side. Remove from pan.

Add lemon juice and wine. Simmer until sauce thickens, about 2 to 3 minutes. Return veal to skillet. Stir in parsley and benne seeds. Blend well and cook another minute or so. Remove from heat and let sit for a few minutes before serving.

RICE AND GRITS

Rice and grits. Rice and grits.
Rice and grits'll give you fits.
Eat 'em hot. Eat 'em cold.
Eat 'em only if you're bold.

Eat 'em when your tummy's queasy.
Eat 'em when they're hot and cheesy.

Rice and grits. Rice and grits.
Rice and grits'll give you fits.

What a charming little ditty we used to sing when we were kids. Grits are made from corn, so I don't know why we lumped them together with rice, but we did. Actually, grits can substitute quite nicely for rice on many occasions.

Rice was originally grown along the South Carolina coast when the colonies were first settled. Rice was a diet staple and much beloved in the Lowcountry. When rice growing became mechanized, the Carolina rice fields couldn't support heavy equipment, so rice growing moved to Arkansas, Louisiana, Texas and California. Happily, rice growing is making a comeback in the Carolinas, although on a very small scale.

Most folks are familiar with boiled rice or converted rice. They've really missed out on the best way to prepare rice—in a rice steamer. It takes a little longer, but the rice really cooks itself and it's foolproof. Using a rice steamer ensures fluffy rice with separate grains.

Rice Steamers

A rice steamer is a variation on a double boiler. It has three parts: (1) the bottom of the steamer is a deep pot, usually 6-qt. capacity; (2) the top of the steamer, an insert pan, has holes in the rim and just below the rim to allow steam from the bottom to enter—the insert should be about 2 inches above water when the bottom is filled; and (3) the top should be tight-fitting so as not to let too much steam escape.

My steamers (I have five) aren't limited to steaming rice. I steam asparagus, broccoli, cauliflower, green beans, squash, even hot dog buns in my "rice" steamers. If you're cooking for a large crowd, you'll be glad to have more than one. It's usually better to make two separate batches of rice rather than double the recipe.

Wear-Ever makes the best—a 6-qt. steamer—but their models can be hard to come by. The Foley Company makes a smaller 4-qt. version that works relatively well. Others are available. You'll probably need to go to a kitchen specialty shop to find one. But I've seen them occasionally in hardware stores. Should you be fortunate enough to find several at one time, buy them all. They make great presents.

If all else fails, use a large double boiler.

Grits

Grits, a classic Southern food misunderstood by most non-Southerners, is not just a breakfast food. It's not the South's answer to hash browns or a substitute for oatmeal. We love grits any time of day, especially when they've been dressed up a bit as I've done in my recipes for Glorified Grits (p. 84), Pan-fried Grits (p. 84) and Shrimp and Grits (p. 49). Like rice, grits are basically a bland food that can be readily flavored by certain ingredients like sharp cheddar cheese. If you've avoided grits up to this point in your life, just cook up a batch and add some cheese and butter. You'll be pleasantly surprised.

Grits have a few other uses you should know about. *Uncooked* grits can be used to remove oily spots from suede. Spread the grits over the spot, rub lightly and let sit for 5 to 10 minutes. Brush grits away. You may need to repeat the process for tough spots. *Cooked* grits will calm an uneasy stomach brought on by excessive imbibing. Enough home remedies . . . let's cook some rice and grits.

Steamed Rice

Once you taste Steamed Rice, you'll wonder how you ever ate it any other way. It takes less than 60 virtually unattended minutes to prepare. My friend Brenda (she's originally from Ohio and didn't know about Steamed Rice) loves the rice steamer I gave her. She says it lets her cook wonderfully fluffy rice every time with no effort. SERVES 6 TO 8.

2 cups long-grain white rice
1¾ cups water, approx.
Pinch of salt

Place rice in top of rice steamer or double boiler. Add enough water to cover rice. Add salt. Fill bottom of steamer with at least 2 inches of water.

Cover and cook over high heat for 30 minutes. Fluff rice with fork to separate. Reduce heat to medium, cover and cook another 15 to 20 minutes.

TIP Rice has been known to stick to pans. For easy clean up, soak pan in cold water for an hour and the rice will rinse right out.

Red Rice

This is the best rice dish in the world—maybe the entire universe! It's unique to Charleston and draws rave reviews every time. The one drawback is that there's no low-calorie way to prepare this. So prepare it only for special occasions. Red Rice is especially good with Southern barbeque, barbequed ribs, pork roast or baked ham. It works well with any kind of chicken or seafood. We even eat cold leftovers. It's a colorful tasty dish that will enhance almost any menu. But if you're not married, don't serve this to a "significant other" unless you're really interested. Once they taste this, it's true love! Just ask Roy. SERVES 6.

2 cups long-grain white rice
8 slices bacon
2 medium onions, chopped
1 red bell pepper, chopped
1 6-oz. can Progresso tomato paste
1½ cups water

1 tsp. sugar
½ tsp. salt
½ tsp. pepper
4 tbsp. bacon drippings

Fill bottom of rice steamer with at least 2 inches of water. Place rice into rice steamer insert.

Fry bacon until crisp then remove from frying pan and set aside. Remove bacon drippings, leaving 2 tbsp. in the pan and reserve the rest. Sauté onions and bell pepper until tender.

Add tomato paste, water, sugar, salt and pepper. Cook uncovered on low heat for 10 minutes, stirring occasionally. Mixture should reduce to slightly more than 2 cups. Add tomato mixture to rice in top of steamer, add bacon drippings and mix well.

Cover and cook over high heat for 30 minutes. Fluff rice with fork to separate grains. Add crumbled bacon. Check water level in bottom of steamer and add more if needed. Reduce heat to medium low, cover and cook another 45 minutes.

Rice Pilau

Pilau is just fancy steamed rice dressed up with a few sautéed vegetables. Many different vegetables can be used—bell pepper, onion, mushrooms, julienned carrots, zucchini, yellow squash, etc. Mix and match vegetables for variety.
SERVES 6.

2 slices bacon
2 cups chicken stock
2 cups long-grain white rice
¼ tsp. salt
3 tbsp. butter
¼ cup onion, chopped
¼ cup red bell pepper, chopped
¼ cup fresh mushrooms, sliced
1 large zucchini, julienned

Fry bacon until crisp and set aside. Add bacon drippings to chicken stock. Fill bottom of steamer with 2 inches of water. Place rice in top of steamer. Add enough stock to cover rice (approximately 2 cups). Add salt. Cover and cook over high heat for 30 minutes.

Meanwhile, in a large skillet, sauté vegetables in butter until just tender.

After rice has cooked for 30 minutes, fluff rice with fork to separate grains, add rice to vegetables and mix well. Reduce heat to low, cover and cook another 10 minutes. Stir in crumbled bacon and serve hot.

■■■■■■■■■■■■■■■■■■■■

Bama's Okra Purlow

Okra is a much-maligned vegetable because if improperly cooked, it can be downright slippery. The secret is to "deslime" the okra by "frying it dry" in bacon drippings or some other oil. Okra "purlow," as my grandmother Bama pronounced it, has a completely unique flavor and will become a favorite of yours before you know it. Who knows—Geechee Gumbo, Gumbo Soup, fried or pickled okra may be next! We like Bama's Okra Purlow with a pork roast or ham.
SERVES 4.

4 slices bacon
2 cups fresh okra, cut into ¼-inch rings
1 cup long-grain white rice
1 cup water
Salt and pepper to taste.

Fry bacon with okra rings until tender and okra juice has been absorbed. Add rice, water, salt and pepper. Mix well and place in top of rice steamer.

Add water to bottom of rice steamer. Cover and cook over high heat for 30 minutes. Reduce heat to medium and cook until dry and fluffy, about 60 minutes.

■■■■■■■■■■■■■■■■■■■■

Hoppin' John

Hoppin' John is guaranteed to bring you good luck throughout the year if you eat at least a tablespoonful on New Year's Day. We don't want to take any chances, so we usually eat ours just after midnight on New Year's Eve. We like it with scrambled eggs, bacon, sausage, shrimp and grits, biscuits, and of course, a little champagne. Of course, it's good any ole time of the year, with or without the champagne. I'm getting hungry just thinking about it! This *Charleston Receipts* recipe is just one of many traditional Low country dishes found in that wonderful cookbook.

SERVES 8.

> 1 cup cow peas (dried field peas)
> 4 cups water
> ½ tsp. salt
> 1 cup long-grain white rice
> 4 slices bacon
> 1 medium onion, chopped

Cook peas in salt water until tender. Let stand in liquid for 1 hour after cooking. (This enhances the flavor.)

Place rice into steamer insert. Add peas and 1 cup of pea liquid to rice, bacon and onion. Add water to bottom of steamer. Cover and cook over moderate heat for about 1 hour until rice is done.

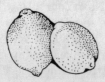

Lemon "Pealoff"

Refreshing and light—no bacon drippings, so it's somewhat more healthful than Red Rice (p. 79), but no less tasty. Garnish with lemon slices and a few sprigs of dill. Serve with Blackened Salmon (p. 96) and Creamed Spinach (p. 58).

SERVES 6.

> 1½ cups long-grain white rice
> 2 tbsp. olive oil
> 1 cup celery, diced
> 1 cup green onions, diced
> 1 clove garlic, minced
> ¼ cup fresh dill, minced
> Salt and pepper to taste
> 1¼ cups chicken stock
> 2 tbsp. lemon juice
> 1 tsp. lemon rind, grated

Stir fry rice in oil over medium heat until golden brown. Add celery and onion and cook until tender, about 3 to 4 minutes. Add garlic and cook for another 2 minutes. Remove from heat and stir in dill. Salt and pepper to taste.

Add water to bottom of rice steamer. Pour rice mixture into rice steamer insert. Add chicken broth, lemon juice and rind. Steam over high heat, covered, for 20 minutes. Fluff with fork, reduce heat and steam another 15 minutes.

■■■■■■■■■■■■■■■■■■■

Sherpa Rice

We discovered this recipe at the Nantahala Outdoor Center restaurant in Bryson City, NC. The food there is just wonderful and the setting, right along the Nantahala River, is beautiful any time of year. I've adapted this recipe for a rice steamer, since boiling rice should be declared illegal. It's already immoral! It's best when served with sautéed vegetables and it's full of protein. A perfect accompaniment for Chicken on the Grill (p. 35). SERVES 8.

1½ cups brown rice
½ cup wild rice
½ cup lentils
¼ cup barley
1 tsp. salt
2½ cups water
3 tbsp. butter
1 medium onion, sliced
1 medium bell pepper, sliced
1 cup sliced mushrooms
½ tsp. garlic powder
¼ tsp. ginger powder
2 tbsp. soy sauce

Place rice, lentils, barley, salt and water in top of rice steamer. Cover and cook over high heat for 30 minutes. Fluff with fork and steam for another 45 minutes. Reduce to low and keep warm.

Sauté vegetables in butter. Add spices and soy sauce. Mix well. Spoon over rice to serve.

Glorified Grits

Grits are another much-maligned Southern delicacy. The secret to grits is to make sure they're not lumpy and they're served piping hot. Of course, doctoring them up a little bit never hurt either. A true grits lover eats them plain or with a little butter. To increase the odds of having nonbelievers try them, you can "glorify" them, dress them up a little bit. They're a great substitute for rice or potatoes. We like these with Salmon on the Grill (p. 57). SERVES 6.

> *2 cups cooked grits (quick grits, not instant)*
> *4 tbsp. butter or margarine*
> *1½ cups sharp cheddar cheese, grated*
> *1 tbsp. garlic powder*
> *2 eggs, slightly beaten*
> *½ cup milk*
> *Heavy dash of cayenne*
> *Salt to taste*

Cook quick grits according to package directions. Pour into large bowl. Add butter, 1 cup of cheese and garlic powder and mix until melted. Add eggs and milk. Add cayenne and salt to taste.

Pour into buttered casserole and top with remaining grated cheese. Bake in 375-degree oven for 1 hour.

■■■■■■■■■■■■■■■■■■■■

Pan-fried Grits (They could change your life!!)

Before you skip this recipe, give me a chance to make a case for fried grits. This can create a very unusual breakfast or brunch dish. It's a wonderful substitute for hash browns. Keep an open mind for just a few minutes, they could change your life! SERVES 6.

> *2 cups cooked grits (quick grits)*
> *4 slices bacon, fried crisp and crumbled*
> *2 tbsp. butter*
> *1 egg, beaten*
> *1 tbsp. water*
> *½ cup cracker crumbs*
> *½ tsp. pepper*

¼ tsp. salt
3 tbsp. vegetable oil

Combine grits, bacon and butter and mix well. Pour into greased 9 × 13-inch baking dish and chill well (at least 4 hours, overnight is better).

Cut cold grits into large squares. Dip grits squares into egg wash (combine egg and water), then dredge in cracker crumbs, salt and pepper combination. In a large frying pan, fry in oil until golden brown, turning only once. Drain on paper towels before serving.

VEGETABLES

It used to be that good fresh vegetables were only available "in season," but that's all changed now and it makes year-round cooking a lot more fun. What were once regional vegetables are now available nationally, even internationally.

Many Southern vegetables appeal to acquired tastes, but offer an alternative to the usual mashed potatoes, green beans or peas found in most regional cuisines. It's not that those vegetables aren't good, it's just that squash, eggplant and okra haven't been fully explored by many people. One possible cause is the care that must be exercised in cooking these vegetables. They can be downright tricky at times and can be unpleasant if improperly cooked. Hopefully my recipes will guide you to very successful results.

I've omitted several really unusual vegetables—chainey briar (wild asparagus), Jerusalem artichokes, dandelion greens, cushaw and tanyah root (elephant's ear). I'm saving those for my next cookbook—*Foods Even Roy Won't Eat!* (It'll be a very short book.)

Geechee Gumbo

While okra is not yet a widely accepted vegetable, it's our favorite especially when it's included in gumbo. Gumbo, which originated in the Carolinas, depends on okra for thickening, unlike Cajun gumbo that uses a roux and filé (ground sassafras leaves) for thickening. Seafood Gumbo (p. 58) uses the Cajun approach. Geechee Gumbo uses the Charleston approach—no roux, no filé.
SERVES 6.

8 slices bacon
2 lbs. fresh okra, cut into ¼-inch slices
2 large onions, chopped
2 35-oz. cans tomatoes, chopped
4 ears sweet corn, kernels cut from cobs
Salt, pepper, thyme and Worcestershire to taste
3 cups Steamed Rice (p. 79)

In a large frying pan, cook bacon until crisp. Remove from pan. Remove half the bacon drippings and set aside.

Add okra and onions to remaining bacon drippings and cook over medium heat until nearly all "okra juice" is cooked out. (Yes, we're "desliming" the okra!!) Add remaining bacon drippings and cook for 1 additional minute.

Place tomatoes and liquid into large Dutch oven. Add okra mixture and corn. Season to taste with spices.

Simmer uncovered for at least 3 hours, stirring occasionally, and add a little water as needed.

Serve over Steamed Rice (p. 79) with bacon crumbled on top.

OPTION Some or all of the following ingredients can be used to augment the basic gumbo recipe.

1 cup sieva beans (teeny baby lima beans)
1 cup shrimp, peeled and deveined
1 cup oysters, select size
1 cup crab meat, picked at least twice for
*   particles*

Add vegetables before simmering begins. Add seafood to hot gumbo 15 minutes before serving.

Zucchini on the Grill

Zucchini on the grill is a surprising veggie! You'll think you're eating really good eggplant. (Not that real eggplant isn't good.) You'll never want to eat boiled zucchini again! It tastes delightful and it's low calorie!

SERVES 4.

6 medium zucchini
½ cup Italian dressing
2 tbsp. butter or margarine

Cut ends off zucchini, then cut lengthwise into quarters. (The zucchini should look like French fries. If the zucchini is very long, cut in half.)

In a nonmetallic bowl, combine zucchini and dressing. Toss well. Allow zucchini to marinate in dressing for at least 30 minutes before cooking.

Place zucchini directly on the grill. Cook for 5 minutes on the first (skinless) side, 5 minutes on the second side and 2 minutes on the third.

Toss with butter or margarine before serving.

TIP Yellow squash can be substituted or added for color, but you won't get the eggplant flavor. I often skewer bell pepper, onions and mushrooms, baste with butter or margarine and cook along with the zucchini. Then everything is mixed together before serving. It's scrumptious and colorful!

TIP You can substitute low-calorie dressing and diet margarine without changing the taste of the dish and save yourself a few calories.

Zucchini Matchsticks

Get your Moha mandolin (p. 11) and a box of Band-Aids! This recipe isn't so dangerous as Cool as a Cucumber Salad (p. 119), but you do need to exercise care. That mandolin blade is sharp! Once you acquire a taste for "plain" zucchini, substitute diet margarine for the butter and omit the cheese. You'll have a truly low-calorie favorite.

SERVES 4.

3 tbsp. butter
1 medium onion, julienned
6 medium zucchini, julienned
Salt and pepper to taste
¼ cup Parmesan cheese, grated
½ cup pine nuts, toasted

In large frying pan, melt butter over moderate heat. Add onion and cook for 2 to 3 minutes, stirring constantly. Add zucchini and mix well. Cook until zucchini is heated through, about 3 to 4 minutes. Add salt and pepper. Sprinkle with cheese and pine nuts then toss well. Serve immediately.

■■■■■■■■■■■■■■■■■■■■■■■

Charleston Squash Pie

This pie doesn't have a real crust, but it has a lot of goodies in it. It's sometimes baked in a pie plate, but I usually use a casserole dish. Of all the recipes in this book, it was the most difficult for me to specify and quantify the ingredients. I never really cook it the same way twice. Here are the basics, so don't be afraid to experiment.

SERVES 8.

3 lbs. yellow squash, cut into ¼-inch slices
6 strips bacon (can be omitted if you must)
1 large onion, diced
1 bell pepper, chopped
½ cup sour cream or low-calorie substitute
2 tbsp. butter, margarine or low-calorie substitute
Salt and pepper to taste
2 cups sharp cheddar cheese, grated
½ cup seasoned bread crumbs

Boil squash until not quite tender, about 10 minutes on high heat. Drain well and set aside in large bowl.

Cook bacon until crisp. Fry onion and bell pepper in drippings until tender. Add crumbled bacon, onions, bell pepper, sour cream, butter or margarine, salt and pepper to squash and mix gently.

In a lightly greased casserole, layer squash mixture, then cheese and repeat until all the mixture is used. Cover top cheese layer with bread crumbs.

Bake in 350-degree oven for 30 minutes until hot and bubbly.

OPTION If you really want it to look like a pie, use 2 glass pie plates. Sprinkle an additional ¼ cup bread crumbs into each pie plate. Spread some cheese on top of crumbs. Bake in oven until cheese melts. Add squash mixture. Add remaining cheese and cover with bread crumbs.

■■■■■■■■■■■■■■■■■■

Yellow Squash Boats

Cute little squash boats are a surefire way to convert nonsquash eaters. This is an unusual presentation, sure to cause a few comments at the dinner table. If there are any leftovers, they're even good cold.
SERVES 6.

6 large yellow squash, cut in half lengthwise
4 tbsp. butter, divided
1 medium onion, chopped
1 bell pepper, chopped (your choice of color)

4 slices bacon, fried crisp and crumbled
2 tbsp. sour cream or low-calorie substitute
Salt and pepper to taste
½ cup sharp cheddar cheese, grated
⅓ cup seasoned bread crumbs

Boil squash until tender, about 10 minutes. Drain well and scoop out flesh without disturbing the skin, leaving a shell of at least ¼ inch.

Sauté onion and bell pepper in 3 tablespoons butter for 2 to 3 minutes. Mash scooped-out squash well and add onions and bell pepper. Add bacon and sour cream. Salt and pepper to taste.

Place squash skins in greased baking dish, fill with squash mixture, sprinkle with cheddar cheese then bread crumbs. Dot with remaining butter and bake in 375-degree oven for 20 to 25 minutes.

Stuffed Eggplant

Eggplant, or Guinea squash, is a South Carolina Lowcountry favorite. We like the stuffed version because it's colorful and tasty.
SERVES 4.

2 small eggplants
2 tbsp. butter
1 onion, chopped fine
1 egg, beaten
¼ cup Parmesan cheese, grated
Salt and pepper to taste
¼ cup seasoned bread crumbs
Butter

Cut eggplants in half lengthwise. Scoop out inside, leaving ¼-inch shell. Cover scooped out eggplant with water, bring to a boil and cook until soft. Drain well. Sauté onion in butter until tender. Add to eggplant. Add egg and cheese. Salt and pepper to taste.

Fill each eggplant half with mixture. Sprinkle with bread crumbs and dot with butter. Place in shallow pan with ½-inch water and bake in 350-degree oven for 30 minutes.

Momma's Potatoes Au Gratin

Momma has done it again! These are the best potatoes au gratin I've ever eaten. The secret is in the cream sauce. This is no low-calorie dish, so go easy on the dessert!
SERVES 8.

3 lbs. Idaho potatoes
4 tbsp. butter
4 tbsp. flour
2 cups Half & Half
1 lb. sharp cheddar cheese, grated and divided
Salt and pepper to taste

Boil whole potatoes in Dutch oven until tender, about 25 minutes. Drain in colander and let cool. Cut into large bite-size pieces.

Melt butter, combine with flour and cook until smooth, stirring constantly. Add Half & Half, a little at a time, and stir over medium heat until mixture thickens. Add ¾ cup cheese and stir well. Salt and pepper to taste.

Combine potatoes and cream sauce and gently mix thoroughly. Pour into a buttered casserole dish and top with remaining cheese. Bake in 350-degree oven until cheese is completely melted and bubbly.

TIP The potatoes can be cut in half before cooking to speed up cooking time, but don't cut any smaller or the results can be mealy potatoes. That won't do!

■□■□■□■□■□■□■□■□■□

Southern Fried New Potatoes

You'll find these potatoes a great substitute for hash browns at breakfast or other potato dishes at dinner. These are particularly good with Momma's Southern Fried Chicken (p. 42) and Creamed Spinach (p. 96).
SERVES 8.

3 lbs. new potatoes
3 tbsp. butter
1 bunch green onions, sliced thin
Salt and cayenne to taste
Dash of paprika

Put potatoes into large pot and cover with water. Bring to a boil, cover and cook until tender, about 20 minutes. Drain well and allow to cool completely. Do not peel! Cut into ½-inch slices.

Melt butter and sauté potatoes and onions over medium heat until potatoes are crispy. Season with salt and cayenne. Add a little paprika for color.

TIP Cook potatoes a day ahead and refrigerate overnight. This ensures ease in cutting and will reduce the chance of crumbly potatoes.

■■■■■■■■■■■■■■■■■

Carolina Corn Pudding

As my friend Mary would say—"this'll make you knock your grandpa!!" Don't ask me exactly what that means 'cause people from Camden, in the South Carolina Upcountry, have always been a little weird. But corn pudding is a wonderful treat and an enduring Southern favorite. We love corn pudding with fried chicken or ham.
SERVES 6.

2 cups fresh sweet corn kernels, cut off the cob
4 eggs, beaten well
2 cups milk
2 tbsp. butter
1 tbsp. sugar
Salt and pepper to taste

Combine all ingredients and blend well. Pour into greased casserole. Place casserole in pan of hot water and bake in 375-degree oven for 35 to 40 minutes.

Stir mixture twice during the cooking time to keep the sides from sticking. Try not to disturb the crusty top too much.

■■■■■■■■■■■■■■■■■■■■■■■■

Edith's Broccoli Casserole (as adapted by Momma)

People who would never touch broccoli before will be begging you for the recipe. Don't give it to them! Make them spend their hard-earned money on the whole shebang. After all, you or one of your loved ones did! Roy's mother created this wonderful dish and my mother adapted it for Charleston tastes. SERVES 6.

1 large onion, chopped
4 tbsp. butter
2 10-oz. pkgs. frozen chopped broccoli
1 can cream of chicken soup
1 cup sour cream or low-calorie substitute
1 8-oz. pkg. garlic cheese
½ lb. mushrooms, sliced
1 8-oz. can water chestnuts, sliced
¾ cup blanched almonds, sliced
Salt and pepper to taste
⅓ cup bread crumbs

Sauté onion in 3 tbsp. butter in large frying pan. Add broccoli and cook until tender. Add soup, sour cream, cheese, mushrooms, water chestnuts and half the almonds. Salt and pepper to taste. Blend well and pour into large casserole.

Sauté remaining almonds in remaining butter then sprinkle almonds and bread crumbs on top. Bake in 350-degree oven for 30 minutes until bubbly.

Meeting Street Artichokes

As you probably have figured out by now, Meeting Street is a pretty popular place in Charleston cooking. Whether it's artichokes, crab, shrimp or whatever else you can dream up, the sherry-cheese-white sauce, though sinfully fattening, is just the thing for a special occasion. Serve with Stuffed Tenderloin of Beef (p. 68), Dijon Pork Roast (p. 25) or Chicken on the Grill (p. 35).
SERVES 6.

4 tbsp. butter
4 tbsp. flour
1 cup milk
4 tbsp. sherry
Salt and white pepper to taste
2 cans artichoke hearts, quartered (not the marinated variety)
¾ cup sharp cheddar cheese, grated

Make a white sauce with butter, flour and milk. (Melt butter, add flour gradually and cook over medium heat until smooth. Add milk slowly and stir until sauce thickens.) Remove from heat and add sherry, salt and pepper. Add artichoke hearts.

Pour mixture into buttered casserole and top with cheese. Bake uncovered in 375-degree oven until mixture bubbles, about 20 minutes.

TIP When making the white sauce, use a wire whisk for stirring after you add the milk. This'll ensure a smooth result.

Creamed Spinach

Popeye would heartily approve of this recipe. The texture of the spinach is silky and smooth. Well, maybe it's not macho enough for Popeye, but Roy loves it. Serve with Momma's Southern Fried Chicken (p. 42) or "Nawlins"-Style Pork Roast (p. 26).
SERVES 6.

3 lbs. fresh spinach
1 tbsp. butter
1 tbsp. flour
1 tbsp. onion, grated fine

¼ cup sour cream or lower-calorie substitute
½ tsp. nutmeg
Salt and pepper to taste

Wash spinach, carefully discarding stems and leaves that are not tender. Cook spinach in large pot of boiling water for only 3 minutes. Drain well.

In large pot, melt butter and add flour, mixing until well blended. Add spinach, onion, sour cream, nutmeg, salt and pepper to taste. Heat thoroughly over medium heat, stirring constantly.

■■■■■■■■■■■■■■■■■■■■■

Vidalia Onions on the Grill

Unfortunately, these wonderful sweet onions aren't available year-round, so you may have to substitute large white onions. Wadmalaw Sweets and Walla Walla onions are great substitutes too. They're usually very mild. Both Vidalia and Walla Walla onions are available via mail order. You'll have to go to Charleston to find the Wadmalaw onions. Anyway, once you have the onions, this is an easy recipe and just requires a little head start on the rest of the meal.

SERVE ONE ONION PER PERSON. (ROY USUALLY GETS TWO.)

1 Vidalia onion
1 tsp. butter, margarine or low-calorie
  substitute
½ tsp. parsley, chopped
½ tsp. Worcestershire sauce
Dash of cayenne
Dash of paprika

Peel onion and cut off top and bottom. Prepare a "cradle" of heavy-duty aluminum foil to hold onion. Cover top of onion with next five ingredients.

Place directly on the grill over medium fire and cook for 45 minutes. (You'll be able to cut this with your fork.)

Edith's Creamed Onions

This is another of Edith's delightful creations. She suggests 2 onions per person, at least 3 for Roy. I must admit I periodically have trouble with this one. Roy's analysis of the situation usually indicates I did not drain the onions well enough. So a word to the wise—drain your onions well!
SERVES 6.

*12 medium white onions, sliced into ¼-inch
  slices*
4 tbsp. butter
4 tbsp. flour
2 cups milk
2 tbsp. sherry
1 tbsp. Worcestershire sauce
Salt and pepper to taste

Boil onions until almost tender, but still crunchy. Drain well!

In a large pot, melt butter, combine with flour and cook until smooth, stirring constantly. Add milk, a little at a time, and stir over medium heat until mixture thickens. Add onions, sherry and Worcestershire, salt and pepper to taste. Pour into casserole and bake uncovered in 350-degree oven for 25 to 30 minutes, until bubbly.

Momma's Carrots and Apples

Here's another of Momma's quick favorites. It's fast, easy and a little different. The sweet and sour sauce makes a lovely glaze.
SERVES 4.

1 lb. carrots, peeled and sliced diagonally
3 tbsp. water
1 tbsp. butter or margarine
3 apples, peeled and sliced
*2 tbsp. sweet and sour sauce (use LaChoy
  Original Sweet and Sour Sauce)*

Put carrots and water into a 10-inch frying pan. Cover and cook over medium-low heat until carrots are tender, about 10–15 minutes. Remove carrots from pan, drain well and set aside. Melt butter or margarine. Sauté apples for 2 minutes. Add sweet and sour sauce and carrots. Cook until glazed and heated through, about 3 minutes.

■■■■■■■■■■■■■■■■

Tomatoes on the Grill

Here's another easy one for the grill. Tomatoes are just perfect for the grill since they contain so much water—they can't dry out. They cook fast and can be very hot, so be careful. If your menu needs a little color, this is the perfect finishing touch. SERVE 1 TOMATO PER PERSON.

    1 large ripe tomato
    1 tsp. butter or margarine
    ½ tsp. basil, chopped
    ½ tsp. oregano
    Garlic powder and pepper to taste

Cut off top of tomato and leave peel intact. Prepare a "cradle" of heavy-duty aluminum foil to hold to-mato. Cover top of tomato with remaining ingredients.

Place directly on the grill over medium fire and cook for 35 minutes.

■■■■■■■■■■■■■■■■

Stewed Tomatoes

Momma used to make this on "cold" winter nights. (During the two "cold" weeks in January, the temperature must have plunged to at least 40 degrees. And to think that in Chicago we've been exposed to windchills of 75-degrees below zero. I seldom needed a winter coat in Charleston.) This recipe can really heat you up, so I suggest preparing it in winter only or turn up your air conditioner and enjoy these hot tomatoes any time of year. SERVES 6.

    4 cups tomatoes, peeled and quartered
    ½ cup Parmesan cheese, grated
    2 tbsp. butter, melted
    2 tbsp. sugar

*4 biscuits, crumbled (use Pillsbury ready-made
  buttermilk biscuits or make Benne Biscuits
  [p. 135] without the benne seeds)
Salt and pepper to taste*

Combine all ingredients in large bowl. Blend well.
Pour into casserole. Cover and bake in 350-degree
oven for 30 minutes. Serve piping hot.

TIP If you're in a hurry, this can also be cooked on
the stovetop in a pot over medium heat for 15 minutes. Stir occasionally so it won't burn.

■■■■■■■■■■■■■■■■■

Aunt Mamie's Sweet Potato Soufflé

Well, Aunt Mamie's done it again! Here's her
favorite way to prepare sweet potatoes.
SERVES 6.

*1 large can sweet potatoes
2 eggs, beaten*

*1 small can evaporated milk (Pet or
  Carnation)
1 scant cup sugar
1 stick butter, melted
1 tsp. vanilla
1 can whole cranberries
¾ cup pecan pieces*

In a large mixing bowl, mash potatoes. Add next six
ingredients and blend well. Pour into 1½-qt. casserole dish. Top with pecan pieces. Bake at 350 degrees
for 30 to 40 minutes. Serve hot.

OPTION Aunt Mamie suggests using fresh sweet
potatoes when you have the time. Substitute 4 large
cooked potatoes.

Sweet Potato French Fries

I f you can't bring yourself to eat Aunt Mamie's soufflé, you'll certainly give this a try. Roy generally isn't overly fond of sweet potatoes, but he loves them prepared as fries. These are great with a little Southern barbeque (p. 21) and cole slaw.
SERVES 6.

2 lbs. sweet potatoes
Vegetable oil
Salt and pepper

Scrub potatoes, dry and cut lengthwise into quarters (leave skin on). In Dutch oven or deep fryer, heat oil to 375 degrees and cook potatoes until lightly golden. Drain on paper towels. Salt and pepper to taste.

APPETIZERS

When we have dinner guests, I don't go overboard on appetizers. There are so many other good things to eat, I don't want them to fill up until we're seated for the main course. But I love "heavy" hors d'oeuvres for cocktail parties and drop-ins. These recipes represent a cross-section of Southern party fare. Many of these dishes were served at our wedding reception. They're perfect for nibbles at brunches too. Many can be made ahead and a lot of them freeze well.

Charleston Shrimp Paste is a sure winner every time. Ham biscuits are a Southern favorite and always very popular with any guests. They always go very fast. You'll think you've made enough and the next thing you know, someone with "Roy" tendencies will be hovering over the table. Then quick as a flash, they're gone and you're heading to the kitchen for replacements. Be sure to stand back when you serve Pickled Shrimp. Your guests will be in a feeding frenzy for sure. Momma's Artichoke Dip is another favorite and so easy to prepare.

Some main dishes such as Meeting Street Crab (p. 55) also work well as an appetizer when served with small patty shells. Use my Pineapple Marinade (p. 65) for tenderloin. Cook until medium rare, slice thin and serve on small pumpernickel and rye rolls with some horseradish sauce. Chicken Kabobs (p. 41) can be made using the cocktail-size bamboo skewers. Ogie's Chicken Salad (p. 117) makes wonderful finger sandwiches. So start planning your Christmas party now or just have a party any ole time.

Charleston Shrimp Paste

This is Roy's favorite appetizer. And to think he probably would have never tasted it if he hadn't met me. Few people outside Charleston have ever tasted this scrumptious delicacy. Serve with Bremner wafers or some other relatively bland cracker, so the shrimp flavor won't have to compete. Save 1 or 2 shrimp to use as a garnish. (It's always fun to see who'll be bold enough to eat the garnish; they always try to do it while no one is watching.) SERVES 6.

    1 lb. shrimp, cooked, peeled and deveined
    ⅔ cup Hellmann's mayonnaise
    ⅓ cup Durkee Famous Sauce
    1 tbsp. dry sherry
    ½ tsp. lemon juice
    Dash of mace
    Sprigs of parsley

Grind shrimp in blender or food processor until very fine meal. Put ground shrimp into mixing bowl. Add remaining ingredients except parsley and mix well until smooth and creamy.

Mound mixture in a small serving bowl. (I like oriental rice bowls.) Garnish with 2 whole shrimp and a few sprigs of parsley. Cover with plastic wrap and chill for at least 2 hours before serving. Serve with your favorite crackers.

TIP Shrimp paste sandwiches are out of this world too! Be sure to cut the crust off white bread and spread a thin layer of mayonnaise on the bread to prevent the bread from absorbing the moisture in the shrimp paste. Serve open-face and garnish each with a sprig of parsley.

NOTE Durkee Famous Sauce is a ready-made sauce with a tangy, mustard-mayonnaise flavor. You can find it in most markets in the mayonnaise or mustard section.

Momma's Artichoke Dip

Quick and easy, can be made ahead and very tasty—so what are you waiting for? Have a party! I recommend serving with Bremner wafers or Carr's Table Water Crackers.
SERVES 12.

> 1 can artichoke hearts, drained and chopped
> fine
> 1 cup Hellmann's mayonnaise
> 1 cup sour cream
> 1 cup grated Parmesan cheese
> Heavy dash of cayenne

Combine all ingredients. Pour into small, lightly buttered oven-proof serving dish. Bake at 350 degrees until mixture bubbles and starts to brown, about 25 minutes. Serve with your favorite crackers or patty shells.

Gone-in-a-Flash Ham Biscuits

This is actually a bit of a misnomer. They'll be eaten in a hurry, but instead of making biscuits, I like to use small ready-made party rolls. They're somewhat easier to work with (biscuits tend to crumble) and they freeze better.
MAKES 10 DOZEN.

> ¼ cup mustard
> 2 tbsp. brown sugar
> 1 2-lb. Hormel ham or other fully cooked ham
> ½ cup Hellmann's mayonnaise
> 3 tbsp. mustard
> Heavy dash of cayenne
> 10 dozen party rolls
> 5 tbsp. butter, melted

Combine ¼ cup mustard and brown sugar. Spread over ham. Place ham in shallow baking pan and heat at 300 degrees until glaze forms, about 30 minutes. Let ham cool and slice into thin bite-size pieces.

Combine mayonnaise, 3 tbsp. mustard and cayenne. Slice rolls into 2 layers. Spread mayonnaise mixture over the inside of both layers. Place 2 or 3 pieces of ham on each roll section. Replace top layer. Brush top with melted butter. Wrap tightly in aluminum foil. Bake at 350 degrees for 25 minutes. Pull rolls apart before serving.

TIP If you decide to make these ahead and freeze them, don't brush with melted butter until you heat them for serving and be sure to double wrap them before freezing.

■■■■■■■■■■■■■■■■■■■■□

Aunt Mamie's Smoked Oyster Log

I don't know where Aunt Mamie has been hiding this recipe, but I got it out of her on a recent trip home. Dealing with the cream cheese can be a little sticky, but a brief refrigeration solves that problem. SERVES 8.

1 8-oz. pkg. Philadelphia Cream Cheese,
*   softened*
1½ tbsp. Hellmann's mayonnaise
1 tsp. Worcestershire sauce
Dash garlic powder
Dash onion powder
Dash salt
1 4-oz. can smoked oysters, drained and
*   chopped*
Dried green onion flakes

Combine cream cheese and mayonnaise and blend well. Stir in next 4 ingredients. Spread cream cheese mixture in a rectangular shape about ¼-inch thick between wax paper. Refrigerate for 30 minutes.

Spread oysters on cream cheese mixture and roll it all up jellyroll fashion. Roll log in green onion flakes. Chill overnight.

Serve with Carr's Table Water Crackers or Melba Rounds.

Christmas Cheese Wafers

These can be eaten any time of year, but I've gotten into the habit of making many batches of these during the Christmas holidays. The funniest story associated with these happened a few years back when I made some unusually spicy wafers (I think I put the cayenne in twice) and took them to the office. That happened to be the day the top brass—the Chairman, President and Vice Chairman—took their annual stroll through the various departments of the bank to wish everyone a merry Christmas. I offered them some cheese wafers. I'll never forget the sight of the three of them racing each other to the water fountain. Needless to say, the Chairman got the first drink and I don't work there anymore.

MAKES 6 DOZEN.

> 8 oz. sharp cheddar cheese, grated
> 1 stick butter, creamed
> ½ tsp. salt
> ¼ tsp. cayenne (more if you dare)
> 1½ cups flour, sifted
> Pecan halves

Combine cheese, butter, salt and cayenne and cream them well. Add flour and knead until smooth and pliable. Divide dough in half and make each into a "log roll" about 1½ inches in diameter. Wrap in wax paper and refrigerate for several hours.

Slice into thin wafers, place on cookie sheet and top each wafer with a pecan half. Bake in 375-degree oven for 10 minutes. Remove from cookie sheet and cool on wax paper. Store in airtight container.

OPTION Substitute benne seeds for the pecans. Sprinkle each wafer with seeds before baking.

Stuffed Mushrooms

You can never have too many stuffed mushrooms. They can be made well in advance and frozen. I love to make things ahead! Then they're waiting for you when you need them. On rainy days I can spend hours and hours in the kitchen cooking ahead and stocking up. There's nothing better than

going to the freezer and having a wide assortment ready for defrosting and heating.
SERVES 10 TO 16.

> 2 lbs. fresh mushrooms
> Stuffing mixture

Remove stems from mushrooms and set aside. Place mushrooms in shallow pan. Chop stems and add to stuffing mixture.

CRABMEAT STUFFING

> 2 tbsp. bell pepper, minced fine
> Mushroom stems, chopped
> 2 tbsp. butter
> 1 lb. crabmeat, picked twice for particles
> 1/3 cup seasoned bread crumbs
> 1 egg, beaten
> 1 tbsp. dried parsley
> Dash of cayenne

Sauté bell pepper and mushroom stems in butter until tender. Combine with remaining ingredients in bowl and mix well. Stuff mushrooms and broil for 10 minutes.

SAUSAGE STUFFING

> 1 lb. hot bulk sausage, crumbled
> Mushroom stems, chopped
> 1/3 cup bread crumbs
> 1 egg, beaten
> 1/3 cup sharp cheddar cheese, grated fine
> 1/4 tsp. sage

Brown sausage in skillet and drain well. Combine sausage and other ingredients in bowl and mix well. Stuff mushrooms and broil for 10 minutes.

■□■□■□■□■□■□■□■□■

Cold Crab Dip

We like crabmeat, hot or cold! This particular recipe is refreshing on those sultry summer nights. Easy—so-o-o-o easy—to prepare.
SERVES 14 TO 16.

> 1 cup crabmeat, picked twice for particles
> 1 1/4 cups Hellmann's mayonnaise
> 1/2 cup sharp cheddar cheese, grated fine

4 tbsp. French dressing
1 tsp. horseradish
Pinch of cayenne
Paprika
Sprig of parsley

Combine first six ingredients and blend well. Mound in scallop shell or serving dish and chill for several hours. Sprinkle with paprika for a little color and top with parsley sprig. Serve with your favorite crackers.

Hot Crab Dip

If you like cold crab dip, you'll love Hot Crab Dip. SERVES 6 TO 8.

1 lb. crabmeat, picked twice for particles
1 can cream of celery soup
½ cup light cream
2 tbsp. butter
2 tbsp. pale dry sherry

1 tbsp. Worcestershire sauce
Salt and pepper to taste

Combine all ingredients. Heat in saucepan over medium heat, stirring constantly until mixture is hot and bubbly. Serve in small patty shells or with Melba Rounds.

Pickled Shrimp

You'll have to shoo your guests from the table or yell "Fire" to get them to leave. They'll be jostling for a prime location like nothing you've ever seen. My friend Mary served these at her wedding and the guests acted like 17-year locusts on a tender, young sapling. Needless to say, Roy was right in there with the best contenders and we have the pictures to prove it. SERVES 6 TO 8, OR ROY.

2 lbs. shrimp, boiled, peeled and deveined
Bay leaves
3 medium onions, sliced thin

PICKLING MARINADE

    1 cup olive oil
    ½ cup pickling spices
    ¼ cup tarragon vinegar
    1 tsp. Worcestershire sauce
    1 tsp. sugar
    1 tsp. salt
    ½ tsp. Colman's dry mustard
    Pinch of cayenne

In a deep bowl, place a layer of shrimp, then bay leaves, then onions and repeat until all shrimp are used.

    Combine marinade ingredients, mix well and pour over shrimp. Cover tightly and chill for at least 24 hours. Drain before serving.

TIP Line a shallow serving bowl with romaine lettuce leaves, place shrimp in the bowl and garnish with watercress and parsley. Serve with toothpicks, then stand back so you won't be trampled.

Benne Nibbles

The benne seed (sesame seed) is guaranteed to bring you good luck just like Hoppin' John (p. 81), so says Charleston lore. Roy loves to munch on these when he has some Jack Daniel's and he is probably one of the luckiest people around. He also believes that eating barbeque at least once a week brings good luck too. (He'll use any excuse.)
MAKES 6 DOZEN.

    2 cups flour, sifted
    ¼ tsp. salt
    ¼ tsp. cayenne
    ¾ cup butter
    ¼ cup ice-cold water
    1 cup benne seeds, toasted
    Salt

Combine flour, salt and cayenne. Cream butter and add to mixture. Add water, a little at a time, and knead until dough becomes smooth. Add seeds and roll out dough to a ¼″ thickness on floured surface. Cut out small rounds, about the size of a quarter. Bake in 300-degree oven for 25 minutes. Remove from oven, sprinkle with a little additional salt if you'd like and cool on wax paper.

Store in airtight container.

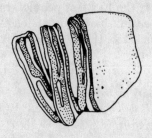

Oysters in Bacon

We just love oysters in any shape, size or form! We also love bacon, although not too often, so this is a match made in Heaven. If you don't like oysters, wrap a stuffed green olive or a whole water chestnut in the bacon instead. Actually, you should probably do all three.
SERVES 12.

48 oysters, drained
24 slices bacon, halved

Wrap oysters in bacon slices. Fasten with a round toothpick. Bake in 425-degree oven until bacon is crisp.

Serve with Cocktail Sauce (p. 61) and Horseradish Sauce (p. 61).

SALADS

Salads are very versatile. They can be the main dish or precede or follow the main dish, and they can be served as part of a "spread," Roy's favorite option. That reminds me of a Roy story . . .

For several summers I prepared a real Southern barbeque for my staff at work. I'd serve Do-It-Yourself Southern Barbeque (p. 21), Red Rice (p. 79), Charleston Squash Pie (p. 91), Momma's Sausage Pudding (p. 26), black-eyed peas, Mrs. Sassard's artichoke relish, etc. Sometimes I'd serve cole slaw and other times I wanted something a little different. One summer I fixed Cool as a Cucumber Salad.

That evening at the barbeque, Roy, who had already had one rather sizable helping, went inside for seconds. He returned with a plate that you wouldn't believe. It was piled a mile high with cucumber salad in the middle, surrounded by barbeque and had some Mrs. Sassard's artichoke relish on top. It was quite impressive and must have weighed tons! Everyone noticed. They all looked at Roy at the same time and started laughing. Roy, being the gracious host that he is, swiveled his chair around, turning his back on everyone and proceeded to eat undisturbed. When he finished, he went back for thirds and everyone followed him into the house to see how much he'd get that time. Now you must understand why his middle name should be All-You-Can-Eat, and why I have learned to cook for a one-man army!

Green Bean Salad

Roy's favorite summertime salad is this green bean recipe that works so well with Southern barbeque and Red Rice (p. 79). The smoky flavor of the ham is very subtly transferred to the beans. It's very refreshing when those hot summer days set in. What perfect picnic fare!
SERVES 12.

 4 lbs. fresh green beans, cut into bite-size
 pieces
 1 red bell pepper, chopped fine
 1 bunch green onions, sliced thin
 1 lb. fully cooked/smoked ham steak,
 cubed

MARINADE
 1 cup red wine vinegar
 1 cup vegetable oil
 3 tbsp. sugar
 2 tbsp. fresh ground black pepper
 2 tbsp. garlic powder
 2 tbsp. oregano

Blanch green beans for 2 minutes. Drain well. Combine with next 3 ingredients in a large nonmetallic bowl.

Combine all marinade ingredients and blend thoroughly. Pour over green bean mixture and stir well. Chill for at least 4 hours. Drain off excess marinade before serving.

■□■□■□■□■□■□■□■□■□■□

Momma's Potato Salad

I've heard many people say that my momma makes the best potato salad they've ever tasted. The recipe seems pretty straightforward and rather basic, so I'm suspicious that she may have forgotten to divulge a secret ingredient. It wouldn't be the first time. I've quizzed her several times and can't trip her up, so this must be it. I usually omit the pimiento (a childhood prejudice) or substitute red bell pepper, so maybe that's why mine just doesn't quite measure up to hers. Whoever thought pimiento could be a secret ingredient!
SERVES 8 TO 10.

5 lbs. potatoes, cut in half and cooked
4 hard-boiled eggs, grated
2 cups Hellmann's mayonnaise
¼ cup Durkee Famous Sauce
½ cup celery, diced
1 small onion, grated
1 small jar pimientos, drained and sliced
Salt and pepper to taste

Cut potatoes into smaller, bite-size pieces. Combine remaining ingredients, mixing well. Gently fold into potatoes being careful not to break up potatoes. Chill for 2 to 4 hours.

■□■□■□■□■□■□■□■□■□■□■□■□

Momma's Shrimp Salad

What a perfect dish for a light lunch. It also makes a dynamite sandwich spread! Serve on a bed of lettuce or in half an avocado with fresh sliced tomatoes, fresh fruit and petite croissants with Mrs. Sassard's blueberry jam.
SERVES 6.

2 lbs. shrimp, boiled, peeled, deveined
3 hard-boiled eggs, grated
½ cup Hellmann's mayonnaise
½ cup celery, diced fine
2 tbsp. Durkee Famous Sauce
2 tsp. sherry

Cut shrimp into bite-size pieces. Combine remaining ingredients. Fold into shrimp. Chill for 2 to 4 hours.

TIP If you're making sandwiches, be sure to spread mayonnaise on the bread first before you spread the salad mixture. This prevents the bread from drawing the moisture out of the salad mixture.

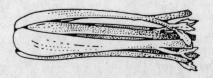

Ogie's Chicken Salad

A longtime family friend who used to do some catering was famous in Charleston for her chicken salad. It's the preparation of the chickens that made the difference. It's intended to be used for chicken-salad sandwiches, but I've stuffed it in tomatoes, avocados, etc. Makes 50 small sandwiches if you choose. Be sure to cut the crust off the bread!

SERVES 8 TO 10.

2 chickens (5 to 6 lbs.)
2 medium onions, peeled
6 stalks celery
Salt and pepper to taste
Juice of 1 lemon
2 cups celery, chopped
8 hard-boiled eggs, grated
1 qt. Hellmann's mayonnaise
½ cup Durkee Famous Sauce

Clean chickens inside and out. Put onions and celery stalks inside chickens. Salt and pepper chickens. Put into large Dutch oven and half cover with water. Cook until tender, about 25 minutes on simmer. Remove pot from heat and let it sit for an hour or so.

Remove chicken from pot and chill overnight. Pick meat from bones, then cut up with scissors. Put cut-up chicken into large bowl. Add lemon juice and toss. Add remaining ingredients. Blend thoroughly and chill several hours.

TIP The secret to Ogie's moist chicken salad is the overnight chilling of the chicken.

Gazpacho Aspic

Y ou may want to try Avocado Dressing (p. 118) on this festive aspic. Aspic is an unusual dish and adds wonderful color to your table. Just plan to make this the night before.

SERVES 8.

2 envelopes unflavored gelatin
½ cup cold water
4 cups V8 Juice
2 tbsp. red wine vinegar

2 small tomatoes, peeled and diced
1 medium cucumber, peeled and diced
1 small bell pepper, diced
1 bunch green onions, sliced thin
¼ cup celery, diced
¼ cup ripe olives, sliced
Dash of Tabasco sauce
Salt and pepper to taste

Soften gelatin in cold water. Heat V8 Juice, add to gelatin and stir until gelatin is dissolved. Add remaining ingredients. Pour into lightly greased 6-cup mold. Chill overnight.

TIP To avoid problems removing the aspic from the mold, fill your sink with hot water and immerse the bottom of the mold for just a few seconds before inverting on your serving platter. Don't leave it in the water for long or your aspic will be watery.

Avocado Dressing

This dressing is well suited for Gazpacho Aspic (p. 117). The creamy sweetness of the avocado is a perfect foil for the tart aspic. Can be used on any green salad.
MAKES 1½ CUPS.

1 large avocado, peeled and mashed
1 tbsp. lemon juice
½ cup sour cream
½ cup light cream
1 clove garlic, minced
1 tbsp. onion, grated fine
1 tbsp. cilantro, chopped fine
½ tsp. salt
Pinch of sugar
Pinch of cayenne

Combine all ingredients and chill well.

Cool as a Cucumber Salad

This is my favorite summertime salad and a great substitute for cole slaw. We often eat this with barbeque. As a matter of fact, Roy creates quite a stir every time he eats this. He's not bashful about filling his plate. Momma says he eats like Charlie Johnson. Charlie was my grandmother's gardener when my mother was a girl. My grandmother Bama always fixed him a hot lunch. She'd keep filling his plate until he said he was full or the food ran out. Charlie never admitted being full. He always had room for just one more helping. Roy should take up gardening.

SERVES 8.

1 cup sour cream or low-calorie
   substitute
2 tbsp. lemon juice
1 tsp. sugar
½ tsp. salt
½ tsp. dried dill weed
Dash of cayenne
4 cucumbers, peeled and sliced paper-thin
1 head romaine lettuce, rinsed and dried

1 red bell pepper, cut into rings
Paprika

Combine first 6 ingredients in large mixing bowl. Add cucumbers, toss to coat and chill well, about 4 hours.

Line large salad bowl with romaine leaves. Pour cucumber mixture into salad bowl. Garnish with pepper rings and sprinkle with paprika.

Fancy Dinner Salad

This salad is a little dressy for Roy's favorites— Southern barbeque (p. 21), Momma's Southern Fried Chicken (p. 42) or Shrimp and Grits (p. 49)— but he likes it with any pork roast or marinated beef, Deviled Crabs (p. 54), Meeting Street Crab (p. 55), Carolina Shrimp Pilau (p. 52), Benne Veal Scallops (p. 73), and so on.

SERVES 4.

1 head radicchio
2 heads Belgian endive

½ lb. mushrooms, sliced
4 oz. blue cheese, crumbled
Seasoned Croutons (see below)
Vinaigrette Dressing (see below)

On individual salad plates, alternate radicchio and endive leaves. Place mushrooms on top of lettuce and then sprinkle with blue cheese crumbles. Top with Seasoned Croutons and a little Vinaigrette.

TIP You can make the salad well ahead of dinnertime. Just don't add the dressing until just before serving.

Seasoned Croutons

Croutons, especially homemade croutons, are the perfect topping for a salad. We also like them in soups. When you have time to make your own, this is a quick recipe.
MAKES ABOUT 1 QUART.

1 loaf French bread, cut into cubes
2 cloves garlic, minced
2 tbsp. olive oil
½ cup Parmesan cheese, grated
1 tsp. fresh ground black pepper

Fry bread cubes in garlic and olive oil until crisp. Drain on paper towels. Sprinkle with cheese and pepper. Allow to cool.

Store in airtight container in cool, dry place.

Vinaigrette Dressing

Get out your Grey Poupon—traditional Dijon or the coarser country version, if you prefer a grainier mustard. This dressing is great on a spinach and mushroom salad too.
MAKES 1 CUP.

¾ cup Puritan oil
¼ cup red wine vinegar
2 tbsp. Dijon mustard

¼ tsp. pepper
¼ tsp. salt
Dash of cayenne

Combine all ingredients and chill well.

■■■■■■■■■■■■■■■■■■■■■■■■

Aunt Mamie's Sauerkraut Slaw

If you'd like something a little different, here it is!
Aunt Mamie has come up with another winner.
Serve with Southern Barbeque (p. 21) or fried
chicken or both.
SERVES 6.

    1 27-oz. can sauerkraut, drained and squeezed
      dry
    1 cup celery, diced
    1 cup green bell pepper, chopped
    1 onion, chopped
    1 2-oz. can pimiento, drained and diced
    1½ cups sugar

½ cup white vinegar
½ cup Puritan oil

In a large bowl, combine first 5 ingredients. In a jar,
mix the remaining ingredients and pour into bowl.
Toss with vegetable mixture, then chill for several
hours.

■■■■■■■■■■■■■■■■■■■■■■■■

Hot Angel Hair Toss

An eye-catching substitute for a green salad that
soon will become one of your favorites. Roy
likes this as an entree as well. He's even requested
it as a late-night snack. It's quick, it's not a lot of
trouble and it's real tasty.
SERVES 6.

    2 tbsp. olive oil
    1 red bell pepper, chopped
    1 yellow bell pepper, chopped
    1 small onion, chopped
    4 cloves garlic, minced
    8 mushrooms, sliced thin

1 tsp. fresh ground black pepper
1 tsp. fresh basil, chopped
1 16-oz. pkg. angel hair pasta
4 tbsp. butter
½ cup grated Parmesan cheese

Sauté bell peppers, onion and garlic in olive oil until tender. Add mushroom slices and cook for another 2 minutes. Add pepper and basil.

Meanwhile cook pasta according to package directions. Drain well and return to pot. Toss with butter. Add vegetable mixture and cheese, then toss well. Serve immediately.

■□■□■□■□■□■□■□■□■□■

Kyle's Wilted Lettuce Salad

No low-calorie salad here—and the cholesterol count must be in the stratosphere. Well, just don't eat this more than twice a year. Kyle got this recipe from her grandmother. Nana concocted this salad before the medical profession found out about saturated fats. Unfortunately there's no substitute for bacon drippings. Serve with broiled fish and eat an oat bran muffin to offset the bacon.
SERVES 4.

1 lb. leaf lettuce, rinsed and dried
5 slices bacon
Bacon drippings
¼ cup cider vinegar
¾ cup water
½ tsp. salt
2 tbsp. sugar
2 tbsp. sour cream
2 hard-boiled eggs, diced

Tear lettuce leaves into bite-size pieces and place into large salad bowl.

Meanwhile, fry bacon until crisp. Remove bacon from pan, crumble and set aside.

In small saucepan combine bacon drippings, vinegar, water, salt and sugar. Simmer for a few minutes, then add sour cream. Heat through and pour over lettuce. Sprinkle eggs and bacon over lettuce and toss. Serve immediately.

SOUPS AND STEWS

We love to eat hearty soups especially on cold Chicago days. Some of these recipes can be served as dinner entrees since they're so full bodied. Gumbo Soup, Carolina Brunswick Stew and Virginia Burgoo are quite filling when served over some Steamed Rice. Bama's Crab Stew is a treat. And False Alarm Chili speaks for itself. Saturday lunch is usually souptime at our house.

Many of these soups freeze well, so make large batches and freeze in pint or quart containers. Then all you have to do is let it thaw out. Rainy cold Saturdays are good for making tons of soup.

Momma's Homemade Vegetable Soup

This is Roy's favorite Saturday lunch in the winter. He loves his veggies and they're especially good in this recipe. This is the only time I use a food processor. It's superb for chopping carrots, turnips, parsnips, etc. (I almost lost a finger using a knife on a parsnip one time.) This soup freezes extremely well and lends itself to many variations with different spices.
SERVES 6.

2 lbs. chuck roast, trimmed of all fat and diced
1 large onion, chopped
3 cups water
Salt and pepper to taste
1 28-oz. can tomatoes with liquid
1½ cups carrots, diced
2 white turnips, diced
2 parsnips, diced
1 lb. string beans, cut into bite-size pieces
2 cups fresh corn
1 cup ketchup
2 tbsp. dried thyme
1 tsp. sugar
Dash of Worcestershire sauce
3 cups Steamed Rice (p. 79)

Boil meat and onion in water with salt and pepper for 30 minutes. Add remaining ingredients and cook over medium heat for at least another 45 minutes. The longer the soup simmers the better. Add a little water if the soup becomes too thick. Serve over Steamed Rice.

TIP For an unusual variation, add 2 tbsp. of herbs from Provence (thyme, basil, savory, fennel and lavender), or add a little Tabasco sauce to spice it up a bit.

Bama's Crab Stew

My grandmother used to make this for my mother when she was a little girl. Then there must have been some generation skipping because it took me 40 years to hear about this one, and I only heard about it since my mother had the flu. She was cooking "a little something good to get her on the road to recovery" when I called to see how she was feeling. I asked her for the recipe and she named the ingredients without any quantities. When I asked for a few specifics she said, "Don't measure, just see what you want it to do. Just don't let it get too soupy. I have no idea, so don't ask me." When I inquired about cooking instructions she said, "Cook it till it's ready." Undeterred, I decided to give it a whirl. Add a tablespoon of sherry to each serving if your fever has broken. Or if you're still sick, remember it's purely medicinal!

SERVES ??? (Y'ALL FIGURE IT OUT FOR YOURSELVES).

- 1 lb. crabmeat (white, special or claw), picked twice for particles
- 2 cups skim milk
- 1 tbsp. butter, margarine or low-calorie substitute
- 6 saltines, crumbled
- Salt and pepper to taste

Combine all ingredients and cook till it's ready!!!

Seriously, gently heat crab, milk and butter in heavy saucepan. (Don't let it boil.) Gradually add saltines a little at a time until desired consistency is reached. If it looks too thick, add a little extra milk. If it looks too soupy, add a few more saltines. How can you go wrong? Salt and pepper to suit your taste.

Add a little sherry to each bowl just before serving. A fresh parsley garnish adds a lovely touch.

False Alarm Chili

This inappropriately named recipe was appropriately named the first time I concocted a pot of chili. It was the strangest thing! It didn't matter what I added to the pot, there was nothing I could do to get the chili to that spicy, hair-burning level I wanted. It was actually a little bland. That is no longer the case, but I still don't know what happened the first time.

SERVES 8.

> 3 tbsp. butter
> 2 large onions, chopped
> 4 lbs. lean ground beef
> 10 tbsp. hot chili powder
> 5 tbsp. mild chili powder
> 3 tbsp. ground cumin
> 3 cloves garlic, crushed
> 1 tbsp. fresh ground black pepper
> 1 tsp. sugar
> 1 tsp. salt
> 1 28-oz. can whole tomatoes with liquid

In large pot, melt butter over medium heat. Add onions and cook until tender and translucent.

Combine meat with next 5 ingredients then add to pot. Cook spiced meat over medium heat stirring occasionally until browned.

Add remaining ingredients and bring to a boil. Reduce heat and simmer uncovered for at least 4 hours—6 or 8 would be better. Stir occasionally and adjust seasonings to suit your taste.

She Crab Soup

No trip to Charleston is complete without a big bowl of She Crab soup! If you can't make it to the Holy City, you can dish it up right in your own home. This soup is very, very rich, much like a thick bisque. Traditionally, only female crabs with roe were used. Male crabs were spared. Doesn't seem fair, but that's life in the Atlantic Ocean. Since I use crabmeat not whole crabs, I substitute hard-boiled eggs for the roe.

SERVES 4.

> 2 tbsp. butter
> 1 tbsp. flour
> 3 cups milk
> 1 cup cream
> 1 lb. white crabmeat, picked twice for
>   particles
> ¼ cup hard-boiled egg yolks, chopped fine
> 1 small onion, grated
> 1 tbsp. Worcestershire sauce
> ½ tsp. salt
> ½ tsp. mace
> ½ tsp. fresh ground black pepper

4 tbsp. dry sherry, warmed
Dash of paprika

Melt butter in top of double boiler. Blend in flour until smooth. Slowly add milk and cream, stirring constantly with whisk. Add crabmeat, egg yolks, onion, Worcestershire, salt, mace and pepper.

Cook slowly for 25 minutes, stirring occasionally. Don't overcook! Don't let it boil!

Put 1 tablespoon warmed sherry in each soup dish, add soup and top with a sprinkle of paprika. Serve immediately.

Gumbo Soup

This is a lot like Geechee Gumbo (p. 89), but it's soupier and has beef in it. Serve over Steamed Rice (p. 79) with Aunt Mamie's Greek Corn Bread (p. 137) or Carolina Cheese Biscuits (p. 135). What a treat!
SERVES 8.

1 large beef bone with plenty of meat
4 qts. water
4 slices bacon
3 lbs. okra, sliced thin
2 medium onions, chopped
2 28-oz. cans tomatoes with liquid
Salt and pepper to taste
4 cups Steamed Rice (p. 79)

In a large pot, cook beef over low heat in lightly salted water until tender, about 2 hours. While that slowly cooks, fry bacon in a large frying pan until crisp, remove from pan, crumble and set aside. Sauté onions and okra in bacon drippings until moisture is cooked out of the okra. (You're "desliming" the okra in this process.) Add the okra mixture, bacon and tomatoes to the beef. Salt and pepper to taste. Cook slowly for another 2 hours, adding a little water if needed. Serve over Steamed Rice.

Carolina Brunswick Stew

Brunswick Stew is the traditional accompaniment for a family-style barbeque in the Carolinas. Corn bread, Momma's Southern Fried Chicken (p. 42), Hush Puppies (p. 139), boiled new potatoes, black-eyed peas, and green beans are usually there too, but Brunswick Stew can be a meal by itself served over Steamed Rice (p. 79). There's some variation by region, so feel free to experiment with your personalized version. Don't forget this freezes beautifully, so making a large batch'll save you time later. It's a great comfort to know something like this is waiting in the freezer.
SERVES 12.

3 lbs. chicken (breasts, thighs and legs)
2 lbs. beef brisket
1 lb. lean pork
2 qts. water, approx.
1 tsp. salt
2 tbsp. red pepper flakes
1 tsp. fresh ground black pepper
2 28-oz. cans tomatoes with liquid
2 cups okra, sliced

2 cups corn
2 cups baby lima beans or sieva beans
2 cups onion, chopped
1 cup potatoes, diced
1 cup green beans, cut into bite-size pieces
¼ cup butter or margarine
Tabasco sauce to taste

Put chicken, beef and pork into a very large stockpot with enough cold water to cover (about 2 qts.). Add salt and pepper. Cover and cook until tender, about 2 hours. Meat should fall easily from bones when done. Discard bones. Shred meat and return to pot.

Add remaining ingredients. Cover and simmer gently for 2 to 3 hours, stirring frequently.

Virginia Burgoo

Kentucky's answer to Carolina Brunswick Stew (p. 129) is Burgoo. Traditional Burgoo is made with mutton, but we prefer beef. Since I adapted this recipe for Roy, a native Virginian and University of Virginia alumnus, I've honored that beautiful state and esteemed institution in this recipe. Even if you're not a Virginian, you'll enjoy this one.
SERVES 8.

> 2 lbs. beef brisket
> 2 lbs. chicken (breasts, thighs and legs)
> Water to cover
> 2 large onions, chopped
> 1 head cabbage, washed and chopped fine
> 2 lbs. potatoes, peeled and diced
> 2 cups corn
> 1 10¾-oz. can crushed tomatoes with liquid
> ½ cup dry white wine
> ½ cup tomato paste
> ¼ cup white wine vinegar
> ¼ cup Worcestershire sauce
> 1 tbsp. lemon juice
> 1 tsp. cayenne
> Salt and black pepper to taste

Put beef and chicken into large stockpot with enough water to cover. Cover and simmer until tender, about 2 hours. Meat should fall easily from bones when done. Discard bones.

Shred beef and cut chicken into bite-size pieces. Return meat to pot.

Add remaining ingredients and simmer for 2 to 3 hours, stirring occasionally.

Oyster Stew

Roy loves oysters and he loves any kind of seafood chowder or stew. This one is particularly easy and tasty.
SERVES 8.

> 1 stick butter
> 2 tbsp. flour
> 2 bunches green onions (separate white and
>   green parts), chopped
> 2 quarts milk
> 2 stalks celery, chopped

1 tbsp. Worcestershire sauce
1 tsp. dried parsley
½ tsp. cayenne
Salt and white pepper to taste
1 qt. oysters and oyster liquor (juice)

Over high heat, make a roux with butter and flour. Stirring constantly, cook until smooth and well blended, about 10 minutes. Add the white part of the green onions and cook until tender.

Heat milk in separate pan and add to roux. Then add green part of green onions, celery and spices. Cook slowly over medium heat, stirring constantly until mixture thickens. Add oysters and oyster liquor and continue to cook until well heated. Don't let it boil!

Serve very hot and lace with a little dry sherry or white wine if you'd like.

Shem Creek Shrimp Bisque

Shem Creek is home base for many shrimp trawlers in Charleston and a great spot for seafood lovers. You can eat in one of the many restaurants along the creek and watch the boats unload their catch. You'll enjoy making this soup for any occasion, but it's especially great as a first course. It's also wonderful for a light supper with a dinner salad and some warm crusty bread. But it's not low-calorie fare. Who's counting calories—certainly, not Roy. SERVES 6.

4 tbsp. butter
1 cup onion, chopped
¼ cup celery, chopped
1 tsp. garlic, minced
2 tbsp. tomato paste
2 tbsp. flour
3 cups milk
2 cups clam juice
½ tsp. basil
½ tsp. parsley
¼ tsp. cayenne
1 bunch green onions, sliced thin

1½ lbs. medium shrimp, peeled and
deveined

In stockpot sauté onion, celery and garlic in butter until tender, about 5 minutes. Add tomato paste and flour and stir until well blended. Add next 5 ingredients and bring to a boil. Reduce heat and simmer for 10 minutes. Add onions and shrimp and simmer until shrimp are pink and opaque, about 6 minutes.

■□■□■□■□■□■□■□■□■□■

Summer Salad Soup

When those temperatures soar in the summer, lettuce wilts without much provocation, so I let my guests drink their salads. This is refreshing and very healthful. Garnish each serving with a dollop of sour cream, a few croutons and a sprig of fresh cilantro.
SERVES 8.

4 large tomatoes, peeled and chopped fine
1 yellow bell pepper, chopped fine
1 green bell pepper, chopped fine
1 cucumber, peeled and chopped fine
½ cup green onion, chopped
2 avocados, chopped
4 cups V8 Juice
4 tbsp. red wine vinegar
4 tbsp. olive oil
1 tsp. salt
½ tsp. fresh ground black pepper

Combine all ingredients in nonmetallic bowl. Chill well.

TIP Make it the day before and let the flavors blend overnight.

BREADS

There are two areas where I don't seem to spend enough time—breads and desserts. Baking breads and preparing most desserts require a lot of precision. I'm really a "taste-and-adjust-as-you-go" cook, and that kind of approach lends itself best to sauces, casseroles and cooking on the grill. But I do have some tried-and-true bread recipes that are always a big hit with our guests.

My Aunt Mamie has two "international" corn bread recipes—one Greek, the other Mexican. It's always tough to decide which one to prepare, so I often prepare both at the same time. My friend Brenda's Award-Winning Onion Shortcake is outrageously good. Carolina Cheese Biscuits are the perfect complement for most soups, gumbos and stews. And they're great for breakfast, dinner and barbeques. When I need a more "formal" bread, I usually let Sara Lee help out. Her Petite All-Butter Croissants are wonderful.

Last but not least is the classic Southern bread—Hush Puppies. These crunchy brown morsels of cornmeal are true Southern fare. We like them with Southern barbeque (p. 21), Momma's Southern Fried Chicken (p. 42) or Fried Oysters (p. 60).

Carolina Cheese Biscuits

Biscuits are great for breakfast, lunch or dinner! We like them with fried chicken or any shrimp dish. They're a lot of fun with grits too. Make several batches at a time, wrap in aluminum foil and freeze. MAKES 2 DOZEN.

> 2 cups self-rising flour (or substitute all-purpose flour and add 1 tsp. baking powder)
> 3 tbsp. vegetable shortening
> ½ cup sharp cheddar cheese, grated
> ¼ tsp. cayenne
> ¾ cup skim milk

Cream flour and shortening with a pastry cutter or fork. Add cheese and pepper. Cream mixture until well blended. Add milk. Mix to a good consistency, soft and moist.

Place dough on floured bread board or wax paper. Flour top lightly. Roll out ½-inch thick. Cut out with small biscuit cutter and place biscuits on cookie sheet. Prick top of biscuits with a fork and bake in 450-degree oven for 12 to 15 minutes, until tops are golden.

OPTION Add ¼ cup smoked ham, chopped fine.

Benne Biscuits

These biscuits are guaranteed to bring you good luck since they're made with benne seeds. If you eat these with Hoppin' John (p. 81) on next New Year's Day, you'll be set for life or at least the next 12 months. MAKES 2 DOZEN.

> 2 cups all-purpose flour
> ½ cup vegetable shortening
> 1 tsp. baking powder
> ¼ tsp. salt
> ½ cup skim milk
> ½ cup benne seeds, toasted

Cream flour and shortening with a pastry cutter or fork. Add baking powder and salt and cream again. Add milk and benne seeds and mix thoroughly.

Place dough on floured bread board or wax paper. Flour top lightly. Roll out ½-inch thick. Cut out with small biscuit cutter and place biscuits on cookie sheet. Bake in 350-degree oven for 8 to 10 minutes.

Brenda's Award-Winning Onion Shortcake

Several years back, my friend Brenda entered this recipe in a contest sponsored by the local newspaper and she won first place. The paper described it as "something tasty and different"—just like Brenda! She has kept this one hidden from me for some time. I just lucked into leftovers the other day. This would be wonderful with chili or a hearty vegetable soup. Actually, it's great just by itself and Brenda swears it'll make men swoon. I won't let her serve it to Roy.
SERVES 8.

>   1 medium sweet Spanish onion, peeled and
>   sliced
>   4 tbsp. butter
>   1½ cups corn muffin mix (or substitute 1 cup
>   self-rising cornmeal and ½ cup flour)
>   ⅓ cup milk
>   1 egg, beaten lightly
>   1 8¾-oz. can cream-style corn
>   4 drops Tabasco sauce
>   1 cup sharp cheddar cheese, grated and
>   divided
>   1 cup sour cream
>   ¼ tsp. dill weed
>   ¼ tsp. salt

Sauté onion slowly in butter until tender and set aside. Combine muffin mix, milk, egg, corn and Tabasco. Place into buttered 8-inch-square pan.

Add ½ cup cheese, sour cream, dill weed and salt to sautéed onions. Spread over corn muffin mixture in pan. Bake at 425 degrees for 15 minutes.

Sprinkle remaining cheese on top and return it to oven for another 25 to 30 minutes, until the cheese browns slightly. Cut into squares and serve warm.

Aunt Mamie's Greek Corn Bread

M y aunt was in an eclectic mood when she dreamed up this recipe. It's a quick and easy recipe since all ingredients are ready-made. Convenience doesn't hurt the taste one bit. And the aroma while it's baking is irresistible.

SERVES 8, BUT YOU'D BETTER MAKE 2 BATCHES.

> 1 pkg. frozen chopped spinach
> 1 pkg. "Jiffy" corn muffin mix
> 1 small onion, grated
> ½ tsp. salt
> 8 oz. cottage cheese
> 4 eggs, beaten
> 1 stick butter, melted

Thaw spinach and squeeze dry. Combine with remaining ingredients and mix well. Bake in buttered 8-inch pan at 400 degrees for 30 minutes.

NOTE If you want to substitute fresh spinach, use one package of spinach. Wash leaves, carefully discarding stems and leaves that are not tender. Cook spinach in large pot of boiling water for only 3 minutes. Drain well and chop.

Mexican Corn Bread

S eems we like our corn bread with an international flavor. Aunt Mamie has another variation, but the approach is a little different—no "Jiffy" mix! It's all from scratch.

SERVES 8.

> 1 cup self-rising cornmeal
> ¼ cup flour
> 2 eggs, beaten

¾ cup milk
¾ cup cheddar cheese, grated
⅓ cup Puritan oil
1 8¾-oz. can cream-style corn
½ bell pepper, diced
2 small hot peppers, chopped
1 medium onion, grated
½ tsp. salt
½ tsp. baking powder

Combine all ingredients and mix well. Pour into greased 8-inch pan and bake at 400 degrees for 25 to 30 minutes.

Carolina Pecan Muffins

Ooey-gooey . . . that's about all needs to be said about these tasty morsels. Of course these'll taste better if the pecans are from South Carolina.

MAKES 1 DOZEN.

1 cup dark brown sugar, packed
1 cup pecan pieces
⅓ cup butter, melted
½ cup self-rising flour (or substitute ½ cup all-purpose flour and ¼ tsp. baking powder)
2 eggs, beaten
1 tsp. vanilla

Place paper baking cups into a one-dozen muffin pan.

In a large bowl, combine all ingredients and mix completely. Fill cups until half full. Bake in 350-degree oven for 25 minutes.

Aunt Mamie's Beer Bread

Since Aunt Mamie doesn't even drink beer, I wonder how she figured out this recipe. Maybe in her younger days she imbibed. Nothing could be quicker or easier than beer bread. The most difficult decision will be what brand of beer to use. I recommend Miller Lite. Be sure the beer is at room temperature.

MAKES 1 LOAF.

3 cups self-rising flour, sifted
3½ tbsp. sugar
1 12-oz. can beer, at room temperature

Combine all ingredients and mix gently. Pour into well-greased loaf pan and bake at 350 degrees for 1 hour.

■■■■■■■■■■■■■■■■■

Hush Puppies

No Southern barbeque would be complete without a batch of these addictive little devils. And to think they got their name from being tossed at hungry dogs to quiet them.

SERVES A BUNCH OF FOLKS. MAKES ABOUT 2 DOZEN.

2 cups cornmeal
¼ cup all-purpose flour
½ tsp. baking powder
½ tsp. baking soda
½ tsp. salt
¼ cup onion, chopped fine
¼ cup red bell pepper, chopped fine
1 egg, beaten
1 cup buttermilk
Vegetable oil for frying

Combine dry ingredients. Add onion and bell pepper. Combine egg and buttermilk. Stir into cornmeal mixture. Mix well.

Drop by teaspoonful into hot oil (375 degrees) in a deep pot. Cook until puppies are golden brown and float on the surface. Drain on paper towels. Serve immediately.

DESSERTS

After a hearty Southern meal, we unfortunately seldom have room for desserts, so I usually cook them only when we have dinner guests.

Nonetheless, desserts have an impressive heritage in the South. The native fruits have always provided an abundance of wonderful ingredients. Georgia may claim to be the "Peach State," but last time I checked, South Carolina produced more peaches than Georgia. Blackberries and blueberries make delicious pies and cobblers. Pecans too have always been a part of fine Southern baking and confections. Pecan pie and pecan pralines are true Southern delicacies.

We usually like something lemony for dessert to clear the palate after all that wonderful Southern food. Lemons and bananas are our favorite ingredients, but there's nothing like a warm piece of pecan pie with a little whipped cream or vanilla ice cream, or maybe a few pralines or gingerbread or a few mint brownies, or . . . see for yourself.

Lemon Ice Box Pie

Quick and easy—just my kind of dessert. But boy is it good! I made a pie for my neighbor Brenda. She hid it from her family in the basement refrigerator and ate the whole pie herself in 2 days. SERVES 6 OR BRENDA.

PIE CRUST

1½ cups graham cracker crumbs
¼ cup pecan pieces, finely grated
4 tbsp. sugar
4 tbsp. butter, melted

Combine all ingredients. Press mixture against bottom and sides of 9-inch pie plate. Bake at 350 degrees for 8 to 10 minutes. Let cool before filling.

FILLING

1 can condensed milk
2 beaten egg yolks, at room temperature
⅓ cup lemon juice

Combine milk, beaten egg yolks and lemon juice to make lemon filling. Blend well until mixture thickens. Pour into pie crust.

MERINGUE TOPPING

2 egg whites, at room temperature
2 tbsp. sugar
1 tbsp. lemon rind, grated

Make the meringue topping by beating egg whites with 2 tbsp. sugar until stiff. Spread on top of filling. Bake pie in 350-degree oven until meringue browns, about 10 minutes. Sprinkle with grated lemon rind. Allow to cool, then chill well before serving.

■■■■■■■■■

Aunt Mamie's Lemon Bars

Aunt Mamie likes to make her lemon bars for "dessert bridge." That's what it's called when you're not energetic enough to make lunch for your bridge group, but you can manage coffee and desserts. An array of Lemon Bars, Momma's Mint Brownies (p. 147) and Pecan Pralines (p. 145) is just perfect for such an occasion . . . or any occasion. MAKES 1 DOZEN.

1 stick butter
1 cup all-purpose flour
¼ cup sugar
3 eggs, beaten
Juice and grated rind of 3 lemons
1½ cups sugar
5 tbsp. self-rising flour
2 tbsp. powdered sugar

Cream butter, flour and sugar. Press into 9 × 9-inch baking pan. Bake for 15 minutes at 350 degrees.

Combine eggs, lemon juice and rind, sugar and flour. Blend well. Pour over warm crust. Bake in 350-degree oven for 25 minutes. Cut when cool, in about 2 hours. Sprinkle powdered sugar on top.

Pecan Pie for Mr. Burns

How my friend Mary's daddy, Mr. Burns, came to be my biggest pecan pie fan is a rather interesting story. I was a guest in their home in Camden, South Carolina, for the Carolina Cup one spring. Her daddy started talking about his pecan trees, so I volunteered to make him a pecan pie if he'd send me some pecans at harvest time. Sure enough, when fall rolled around, he sent a parcel of pecans. I enlisted the help of two of my co-workers to shell the pecans. I had to promise them dinner and that naturally included a little wine. After dinner we sat on the living room floor and started the shelling process. I apparently didn't appreciate my "helpers" condition. Unbeknownst to me, they were occasionally eating the pecan meats and putting the shells into the bowl. Not noticing the shells in the pecan pieces, I made the pie and mailed it to Mary's daddy. Next thing I heard, there was talk of his visits to the dentist. I've mailed him several pies since then and I always pick through the pecans at least 3 times. He always writes me the dearest thank you notes and there's usually an indication that no dental work was required this time.

MAKES 1 PIE.

1 cup sugar
1 cup dark Karo syrup
1 tbsp. butter, melted
1 tsp. vanilla
3 eggs, lightly beaten
1½ cups pecan halves
1 unbaked 9-inch pie crust
0 pecan shells

Combine sugar, Karo syrup, butter and vanilla. Add eggs, then add pecans. Blend well. Pour into pie crust and bake in 375-degree oven for 45 minutes. Serve warm with whipped cream or vanilla ice cream.

████████████████████████

Pecan Pralines

Get your sweet tooth ready for this truly Southern confection. They're addictive!

MAKES 3 DOZEN.

3 cups sugar
1 cup evaporated milk

⅔ cup light Karo syrup
2 tbsp. butter
1 tsp. vanilla
3 cups pecan pieces

Place sugar, milk, syrup and butter into a large saucepan. Heat to boiling, stirring constantly. Reduce to medium heat and cook to a soft ball stage (238 degrees—you'll need a candy thermometer for this).

Remove from heat, add vanilla and pecans and beat until mixture is creamy and begins to thicken. Drop by tablespoonfuls onto wax paper immediately.

Blueberries Jubilee

Some of the finest blueberries are grown in Burgaw, North Carolina. We drive through Burgaw each summer on our annual Southern trek. I like to get some blueberries for Momma. We like blueberry pancakes, but we love Blueberries Jubilee. As an option, this recipe also works well for blackberries, raspberries and cherries.
SERVES 6.

> *2 cups fresh or frozen blueberries, thawed*
> *2 tsp. cornstarch*
> *2 tbsp. lemon juice*
> *2 tbsp. sugar*
> *½ cup water*
> *⅓ cup brandy*
> *Vanilla ice cream*

Mash 1 cup berries in a saucepan. Combine cornstarch and lemon juice. Blend until cornstarch dissolves. Add to saucepan. Add sugar, water and half the brandy to the blueberries. Bring to a boil, then reduce heat and cook until mixture thickens and becomes clear. Add remaining berries and heat through.

In a separate saucepan, warm remaining brandy. Pour over berry mixture and ignite. When flames subside, spoon over individual servings of ice cream.

TIP The brandy must be warmed before pouring over the berries or it won't ignite.

Blackberry Cobbler

There's nothing better than a piping hot cobbler made with fresh blackberries. Top with vanilla ice cream.
SERVES 6.

FILLING
> *3 cups fresh or frozen blackberries, thawed*
> *2 tsp. cornstarch*
> *2 tbsp. lemon juice*
> *¼ cup sugar*
> *½ cup water*
> *1 tbsp. all-purpose flour*

Mash 1 cup berries in a saucepan. Combine cornstarch and lemon juice. Blend until cornstarch dissolves. Add to saucepan. Add sugar, water and flour. Bring to a boil, then reduce heat and cook until mixture thickens. Add remaining berries. Mix well, then pour into 8 × 8-inch glass baking dish.

CRUST

>1 cup all-purpose flour
>1 tsp. baking powder
>¼ tsp. salt
>1 tbsp. sugar
>6 tbsp. chilled butter, divided
>⅓ cup milk

Sift flour, baking powder and salt into a bowl. Add sugar. Cut in 5 tbsp. butter. Add milk all at once. Stir with a fork until well blended. (Mixture should readily pull away from sides of bowl.) Place dough on floured surface. Knead gently, folding 8 to 10 times. Flour top lightly. Roll out with rolling pin about ⅓-inch thick. Spread dough over berry mixture. Remove any excess dough, then seal edges against dish. Brush with 1 tbsp. melted butter, then prick the dough with a fork several times.

Bake for 30 minutes in 425-degree oven.

Top each serving with a scoop of vanilla ice cream.

Momma's Mint Brownies

Momma loves shortcuts and so do I. Why reinvent the wheel when you can augment or adapt a good basic recipe. The Betty Crocker mix is a great start for this brownie recipe. Several of Momma's friends have tried their "scratch" brownie recipes, but agree that Betty seems to work best. My Momma's Mint Brownies always seemed to taste better than my version of her recipe. I recently discovered why. She "forgot" to tell me about the chocolate chips. While I was home in Charleston for a visit, the local newspaper said they were looking for good brownie recipes. So I sat down and typed up Momma's. I gave it to her to review and she said, "Where are the chocolate chips?" I said, "What chocolate chips? What else is missing?" She assures me

the recipe is now complete. It better be, since the paper selected hers for publication.
SERVES 12.

> 1 pkg. Betty Crocker walnut brownie mix
> ¾ cup pecan pieces
> ½ cup semi-sweet chocolate chips
> 1 pkg. Andes creme de menthe mint wafers

Mix brownies according to package directions. Add pecans and chocolate chips. Pour into greased (bottom only) shallow 9 × 13-inch baking pan. Bake at 350 degrees for 25 minutes.

Meanwhile, in top of double boiler, melt the Andes mints. Once brownies are done spread melted mints on top. Let brownies cool in pan for 2 hours. Refrigerate 5 to 10 minutes to set topping. Cut into squares.

Gingerbread Squares

Gingerbread has always been one of Roy's favorites. It can look a little strange for a grown man to eat gingerbread people, so I usually prepare this grown-up version. The lemon sauce is an option I usually reserve for company.
SERVES 8.

> ½ cup sugar
> 1 stick butter
> 2 eggs, beaten slightly
> ½ cup dark molasses
> 1½ cups all-purpose flour
> 1 tsp. baking soda
> 1 tbsp. ginger
> 1 tsp. cinnamon
> 1 tsp. nutmeg
> ½ cup water

Cream butter and sugar. Add eggs and mix well. Add molasses. Sift flour, soda and spices and fold into sugar mixture, adding water a little at a time. Mixture should be moist and well blended.

Bake in greased shallow pan at 350 degrees for 30 minutes. Cut into squares and serve with lemon sauce if you're having company for dinner.

GINGERBREAD LEMON SAUCE
½ cup sugar
4 tsp. cornstarch
1 cup hot water
1 egg yolk, beaten
3 tbsp. lemon juice
2 tsp. grated lemon rind
1 tbsp. butter

In a saucepan combine sugar and cornstarch. Add hot water and blend until smooth. Cook over high heat, stirring constantly until mixture thickens. Reduce heat and cook another 5 minutes or so. Remove from heat. Add a little of the hot mixture to the egg yolk, blend and return it to the saucepan. Mix well and cook another 2 minutes. Add lemon juice, rind and butter. Cook over high heat until mixture becomes thick and clear. Serve over warm gingerbread.

Sour Cream Pound Cake

Don't substitute margarine for butter in this one. It'll really change the texture of the cake, not to mention the taste. Serve with fresh raspberries and whipped cream if you really want to splurge.
SERVES 8.

3 sticks butter
3 cups sugar
6 eggs, separated
¼ tsp. baking soda
3 cups all-purpose flour, sifted
1 cup sour cream
2 tsp. vanilla

Cream butter and sugar. Stir in egg yolks. Add soda to flour. Add flour, sour cream and vanilla to butter mixture. Beat egg whites until stiff. Gently fold egg whites into mixture.

Pour batter into large tube pan that has been greased and lightly floured. Bake at 300 degrees until a toothpick inserted at the center comes out clean, about 1½ to 2 hours. Let cool for 15 minutes before removing from the pan. Serve warm.

████████████████████████████

Heath Bar Toffee Cake

This is really easy, but no one will ever know. That does assume you have an electric mixer. Have you ever tried to whip cream by hand with a wire whisk? It's a nasty experience!
SERVES 8.

1 pt. heavy whipping cream
1 small can Hershey's Genuine Chocolate
    Flavor Syrup
1 white angel food cake, cut into 3 layers
8 Heath toffee bars, crumbled

Whip cream until stiff. Add all but 3 tbsp. chocolate syrup and beat until mixture is well blended and mounds.

Frost bottom layer with a quarter of the whipped cream mixture. Sprinkle with a quarter of the Heath bar pieces. Repeat for remaining layers. Frost sides of cake. Drizzle remaining 3 tbsp. chocolate syrup down side of cake. Sprinkle with remaining Heath bar pieces. Chill overnight.

TIP You'd better buy a few extra Heath bars. They can disappear quickly while you're making this, especially if Roy's around.

████████████████████████████

Banana Pudding

A lot of barbeque places specialize in banana pudding. It's the dessert of choice after you've made a total pig of yourself. I am always amazed how we can manage even a few bites of banana pudding. One day we'll skip the barbeque and eat just the pudding. Not too likely!
SERVES 6 TO 8.

¾ cup sugar
⅓ cup flour
⅛ tsp. salt

4 eggs, separated and at room temperature
2 cups milk
½ tsp. vanilla
60 to 70 vanilla wafers
6 medium ripe bananas, sliced

In top of double boiler, combine ½ cup sugar with flour and salt. Add egg yolks and milk and blend well. Cook over boiling water, stirring constantly, until mixture thickens. Reduce heat and cook another 5 minutes or so. Remove custard mixture from heat and add vanilla.

Line the bottom of a 1½-quart baking dish with vanilla wafers then banana slices. Cover with a thin layer of the custard mixture. Repeat layers of vanilla wafers, banana slices and custard twice more. Add vanilla wafers around the sides of the dish.

Meringue Topping

Make the meringue topping by beating egg whites with the remaining ¼ cup sugar until stiff. Spread on top of pudding. Bake in 350-degree oven until meringue browns, about 10 minutes. Allow to cool, then chill well before serving.

Mrs. Terrell's Fudge Pie

Get the Clearasil ready! This is a chocoholic's delight! If you want a few extra calories, top with a little whipped cream. Aw, what the heck! SERVES 6.

⅓ cup butter
2½ squares unsweetened baking chocolate
4 eggs, beaten
2 cups sugar
¼ tsp. salt
1 tsp. vanilla

⅔ cup pecan pieces
1 unbaked 9-inch pie crust

In top of double boiler, melt butter and chocolate. Let mixture cool slightly.

Meanwhile combine eggs, sugar, salt and vanilla. Add melted butter and chocolate mixture. Add pecans, mix well and pour into pie crust. Bake at 350 degrees for 40 minutes.

Index

Appetizers
  Aunt Mamie's Smoked Oyster Log, 107
  Benne Nibbles, 111–12
  Charleston Shrimp Paste, 105
  Christmas Cheese Wafers, 108
  Cold Crab Dip, 109–10
  Gone-in-a-Flash Ham Biscuits, 106–7
  Hot Crab Dip, 110
  Momma's Artichoke Dip, 106
  Oysters in Bacon, 112
  Pickled Shrimp, 110–11
  Stuffed Mushrooms, 108–9
    Crabmeat, 109
    Sausage, 109

Aunt Mamie's Beer Bread, 138–39
Aunt Mamie's Greek Corn Bread, 137
Aunt Mamie's Lemon Bars, 143–44
Aunt Mamie's Sauerkraut Slaw, 121
Aunt Mamie's Smoked Oyster Log, 107
Aunt Mamie's Sweet Potato Soufflé, 100
Avocado Dressing, 118

Bama's Crab Stew, 126
Bama's Okra Purlow, 81
Banana Pudding, 150–51
Beef
  Beef and Pea Pods, 70–71
  Beef Marinades

    Gravy from Marinade, 66–67
    Italian, 66
    Pineapple, 65–66
  Beef on the Grill, 67
  Blackened Steaks, 69
  Gumbo Soup, 128
  Steak Salad, 69–70
  Stuffed Tenderloin of Beef, 68
Benne Biscuits, 135–36
Benne Nibbles, 111–12
Benne Veal Scallops, 73
Biscuits
  Benne Biscuits, 135–36
  Carolina Cheese Biscuits, 135
  Gone-in-a-Flash Ham Biscuits, 106–7

Blackberry Cobbler, 146–47
Blackened Salmon, 58
Blackened Steaks, 69
Blueberries Jubilee, 146
Boucanier Barbecue sauce, 13, 36
Breads
    Aunt Mamie's Beer Bread, 138–39
    Aunt Mamie's Greek Corn Bread,
        137
    Benne Biscuits, 135–37
    Brenda's Award-Winning Onion
        Shortcake, 136–37
    Carolina Cheese Biscuits, 135
    Carolina Pecan Muffins, 138
    Hush Puppies, 139
    Mexican Corn Bread, 137–38
Brenda's Award-Winning Onion
    Shortcake, 136–37

Carolina Brunswick Stew, 129
Carolina Cheese Biscuits, 135
Carolina Corn Pudding, 94–95
Carolina Crab Cakes, 55–56
Carolina Gold, 22
Carolina Heat, 50
Carolina Pecan Muffins, 138

Carolina Shrimp Pilau, 52–53
Charleston Shrimp Paste, 105
Charleston Squash Pie, 91–92
Chicken
    Chicken and Broccoli, 38–40
    Chicken Kabobs, 41
    Chicken on the Grill, 35–37
        Barbeque, 36
        Cajun, 36
        Greek, 36
        Hawaiian, 36
        Herb, 36
        Hickory, 36
        Lemon Garlic, 35
        Rosemary, 36–37
    Chicken Spoleto, 38
    Chicken What's-It-to-Ya, 40
    Mary's Special Chicken, 37
    Momma's Chicken and Wild Rice,
        33–34
    Momma's Southern Fried Chicken,
        42
    Ogie's Chicken Salad, 117
Christmas Cheese Wafers, 108
Cocktail Sauce, 61
Cold Crab Dip, 109–10

Cool as a Cucumber Salad, 119
Cornish Game Hen on the Grill,
    34–35
Crab
    Bama's Crab Stew, 126
    Carolina Crab Cakes, 55–56
    Cold Crab Dip, 109–10
    Deviled Crabs, 54–55
    Fried Soft Shell Crabs, 62
    Hot Crab Dip, 110
    Meeting Street Crab, 55
    She Crab Soup, 127–28
    Stuffed Mushrooms Crabmeat, 109
Creamed Spinach, 96–97

Desserts
    Aunt Mamie's Lemon Bars, 143–44
    Banana Pudding, 150–51
    Blackberry Cobbler, 146–47
    Blueberries Jubilee, 146
    Gingerbread Squares, 148–49
    Heath Bar Toffee Cake, 150
    Lemon Ice Box Pie, 143
    Momma's Mint Brownies, 147–48
    Mrs. Terrell's Fudge Pie, 151–52
    Pecan Pie for Mr. Burns, 144–45

Pecan Pralines, 145
Sour Cream Pound Cake, 149–50
Deviled Crabs, 54–55
Dijon Pork Roast, 25–26
Do-It-Yourself Southern Barbeque, 21
Dry Rubbed Ribs, 23–24

Easy Herb Stuffing Mix, 45
Edith's Broccoli Casserole, 95
Edith's Creamed Onions, 98

False Alarm Chili, 126–27
Fancy Dinner Salad, 119–20
Fish
Blackened Salmon, 58
Salmon on the Grill, 57
Seafood Gumbo, 58–59
Flexible Bread Dressing, 46
Fried Soft Shell Crabs, 62

Gazpacho Aspic, 117–18
Geechee Gumbo, 89
Gingerbread Squares, 148–49
Glorified Grits, 84
Golden Fried Oysters, 60–61
Gone-in-a-Flash Ham Biscuits, 106–07

Gravy from Marinade, 66–67
Green Bean Salad, 115
Grits
Glorified Grits, 84
Pan-fried Grits, 84–85
Shrimp and Grits, 49
Gumbo Soup, 128

Heath Bar Toffee Cake, 150
Heavenly Pig Pasta, 29
Hoppin' John, 81–82
Horseradish Sauce, 61
Hot Angel Hair Toss, 121–22
Hot Crab Dip, 110
Hush Puppies, 139

Italian Marinade, 66
Italian Sausage Sauce, 28–29

Kyle's Romp in the Hay, 27–28
Kyle's Wilted Lettuce Salad,
122

Lemon Ice Box Pie, 143
Lemon "Pealoff," 82–83
Lowcountry Shrimp, 51–52

Mary's Special Chicken, 37
Maurice's Gourmet Barbeque Sauces,
13
Meeting Street Artichokes, 96
Meeting Street Crab, 55
Melvin's Southern Barbecue sauce, 13
Mexican Corn Bread, 137–38
Moha Mandolin, 11
Momma's Artichoke Dip, 106
Momma's Carrots and Apples, 98
Momma's Chicken and Wild Rice,
33–34
Momma's Homemade Vegetable
Soup, 125
Momma's Mint Brownies, 147–48
Momma's Potato Salad, 115–16
Momma's Potatoes Au Gratin, 93–94
Momma's Sausage Pudding, 26–27
Momma's Shrimp Salad, 116
Momma's Southern Fried Chicken,
42
Mrs. Sassard's relishes, 13
Mrs. Terrell's Fudge Pie, 151–52

"Nawlins"-Style Pork Roast, 26

Ogie's Chicken Salad, 117
Okra
    Bama's Okra Purlow, 81
    Geechee Gumbo, 89
    Gumbo Soup, 128
    Seafood Gumbo, 58–59
Our Very Best Bar-B-Q Ribs, 22–23
Oysters
    Aunt Mamie's Smoked Oyster Log,
        107
    Golden Fried Oysters, 60–61
    Oyster Stew, 130–31
    Oysters in Bacon, 112
    Scalloped Oysters, 60

Panfried Grits, 84–85
Pecan Pie for Mr. Burns, 144–45
Pecan Pralines, 145
Pickled Shrimp, 110–11
Pineapple Marinade, 65
Pork
    Carolina Gold, 22
    Dijon Pork Roast, 25–26
    Do-It-Yourself Southern Barbeque,
        21
    Dry Rubbed Ribs, 23–24

Gone-in-a-Flash Ham Biscuits,
    106–7
Heavenly Pig Pasta, 29
Italian Sausage Sauce, 28–29
Kyle's Romp in the Hay, 27–28
Momma's Sausage Pudding, 26–27
"Nawlins"-Style Pork Roast, 26
Our Very Best Bar-B-Q Ribs, 22–23
Stuffed Mushrooms Sausage, 109
Stuffed Pork Chops, 24–25
Poultry
Chicken and Broccoli, 38–40
Chicken Kabobs, 41
Chicken on the Grill, 35–37
    Barbeque, 36
    Cajun, 36
    Greek, 36
    Hawaiian, 36
    Herb, 36
    Hickory, 36
    Lemon Garlic, 35
    Rosemary, 36–37
Chicken Spoleto, 38
Chicken What's-It-to-Ya, 40
Cornish Game Hen on the Grill,
    34–35

Easy Herb Stuffing Mix, 45
Flexible Bread Dressing, 46
Mary's Special Chicken, 37
Momma's Chicken and Wild Rice,
    33–34
Momma's Southern Fried Chicken,
    42
Smoky Turkey Gravy, 45
Thanksgiving Turkey on the Grill,
    43–44

Red Rice, 79–80
Red Shrimp Pie, 53
Rice
    Bama's Okra Purlow, 81
    Carolina Shrimp Pilau,
        52–53
    Hoppin' John, 81–82
    Lemon "Pealoff," 82–83
    Momma's Chicken and Wild Rice,
        33–34
    Red Rice, 79–80
    Rice Pilau, 80–81
    Rice Steamer, 11, 76
    Sherpa Rice, 83
    Steamed Rice, 79

Salads
  Aunt Mamie's Sauerkraut Slaw, 121
  Avocado Dressing, 118
  Cool as a Cucumber Salad, 119
  Fancy Dinner Salad, 119–20
  Gazpacho Aspic, 117–18
  Green Bean Salad, 115
  Hot Angel Hair Toss, 121–22
  Kyle's Wilted Lettuce Salad, 122
  Momma's Potato Salad, 115–16
  Momma's Shrimp Salad, 116
  Ogie's Chicken Salad, 117
  Seasoned Croutons, 120
  Steak Salad, 69–70
  Vinaigrette Dressing, 120–21
Salmon on the Grill, 57
Sausage
  Heavenly Pig Pasta, 29
  Italian Sausage Sauce, 28–29
  Momma's Sausage Pudding, 26–27
  Stuffed Mushrooms Sausage, 109
Scalloped Oysters, 60
Scallops "Scallopini," 56–57

Seafood
  Aunt Mamie's Smoked Oyster Log, 107
  Bama's Crab Stew, 126
  Blackened Salmon, 58
  Carolina Crab Cakes, 55–56
  Carolina Heat, 50
  Carolina Shrimp Pilau, 52–53
  Charleston Shrimp Paste, 105
  Cocktail Sauce, 61
  Cold Crab Dip, 109–10
  Deviled Crabs, 54–55
  Fried Soft Shell Crabs, 62
  Golden Fried Oysters, 60–61
  Horseradish Sauce, 61
  Hot Crab Dip, 110
  Lowcountry Shrimp, 51–52
  Meeting Street Crab, 55
  Momma's Shrimp Salad, 116
  Oyster Stew, 130–31
  Oysters in Bacon, 112
  Pickled Shrimp, 110–11
  Red Shrimp Pie, 53
  Salmon on the Grill, 57
  Scalloped Oysters, 60
  Scallops "Scallopini," 56–57
  Seafood Gumbo, 58–59
  Seasoned Croutons, 120
  She Crab Soup, 127–28
  Shem Creek Shrimp Bisque, 131–32
  Shrimp and Grits, 49
  Spicy Shrimp Sauté, 50–51
  Stuffed Mushrooms Crabmeat, 109
  White Shrimp Pie, 53–54
Seasoned Croutons, 120
She Crab Soup, 127–28
Sherpa Rice, 83
Shrimp
  Carolina Shrimp Pilau, 52–53
  Charleston Shrimp Paste, 105
  Lowcountry Shrimp, 51–52
  Momma's Shrimp Salad, 116
  Pickled Shrimp, 110–11
  Red Shrimp Pie, 53
  Seafood Gumbo, 58–59
  Shem Creek Shrimp Bisque, 131–32
  Shrimp and Grits, 49
  Spicy Shrimp Sauté, 50–51
  White Shrimp Pie, 53–54
Smoky Turkey Gravy, 45
Soups and Stews
  Bama's Crab Stew, 126

Carolina Brunswick Stew, 129
False Alarm Chili, 126–27
Gumbo Soup, 128
Momma's Homemade Vegetable
    Soup, 125
Oyster Stew, 130–31
She Crab Soup, 127–28
Shem Creek Shrimp Bisque, 131–32
Summer Salad Soup, 132
Virginia Burgoo, 130
Sour Cream Pound Cake, 149–50
Southern Barbeque, See
    Do-It-Yourself Southern
    Barbeque
Southern Fried New Potatoes, 94
Spicy Shrimp Sauté, 50–51
Steak Salad, 69–70
Steamed Rice, 79
Stewed Tomatoes, 99–100
Stuffed Eggplant, 93
Stuffed Mushrooms, 108–9
    Crabmeat, 109
    Sausage, 109
Stuffed Pork Chops, 24–25
Stuffed Tenderloin of Beef, 68

Stuffed Veal Chops on the Grill,
    72–73
Summer Salad Soup, 132
Sweet Potato French Fries, 101

Thanksgiving Turkey on the Grill,
    43–44
Tomatoes on the Grill, 99

Veal
    Benne Veal Scallops, 73
    Stuffed Veal Chops on the Grill,
        72–73
    Veal, Mushrooms and Bell Peppers,
        71–72
Vegetables
    Aunt Mamie's Sweet Potato Soufflé,
        100
    Carolina Corn Pudding, 94–95
    Charleston Squash Pie, 91–92
    Creamed Spinach, 96–97
    Edith's Broccoli Casserole, 95
    Edith's Creamed Onions, 98
    Geechee Gumbo, 89
    Meeting Street Artichokes, 96

Momma's Carrots and Apples,
    98–99
Momma's Potatoes Au Gratin,
    93–94
Southern Fried New Potatoes, 94
Stewed Tomatoes, 99–100
Stuffed Eggplant, 93
Sweet Potato French Fries, 101
Tomatoes on the Grill, 99
Vidalia Onions on the Grill, 97
Yellow Squash Boats, 92
Zucchini Matchsticks, 90–91
Zucchini on the Grill, 90
Vidalia Onions on the Grill, 97
Vinaigrette Dressing, 120–21
Virginia Burgoo, 130

White Shrimp Pie, 53–54
Wisconsin Wilderness Barbecue
    sauces, 13

Yellow Squash Boats, 92

Zucchini Matchsticks, 90–91
Zucchini on the Grill, 90